Lamar Dodd

A Retrospective Exhibition

The High Museum of Art, Atlanta   *September 27, 1970 — November 1, 1970*

The Georgia Museum of Art, Athens   *November 15, 1970 — January 15, 1971*

Lamar Dodd

A Retrospective Exhibition   *The High Museum of Art*

In collaboration with the Georgia Museum of Art   *The University of Georgia, Athens*

The University of Georgia Press   Athens, Georgia

Seventy-five hundred copies of this publication
were printed by Litho-Krome Company, Columbus, Georgia
for the University of Georgia Press in 1970.
Type is Monotype Bembo 270.
Composition by The J.W. Ford Company, Atlanta, Georgia.
Cover stock is 10 pt. Kromekote Cover (CC1S) and 70 lb. Carnival Offset Gray
Text stock is 100 lb. Weyerhaeuser Kashmir Text

Published in the United States of America in 1970 by
The University of Georgia Press, Athens, Georgia 30601

Designed by Ronald Arnholm

Research by Betty C. Cabin

John W. Gardner   Lamar Dodd is a great American. He is an immensely gifted artist and
a superb human being. He has a keen eye and a generous heart.
Both the man and his work express the best that this nation can produce.

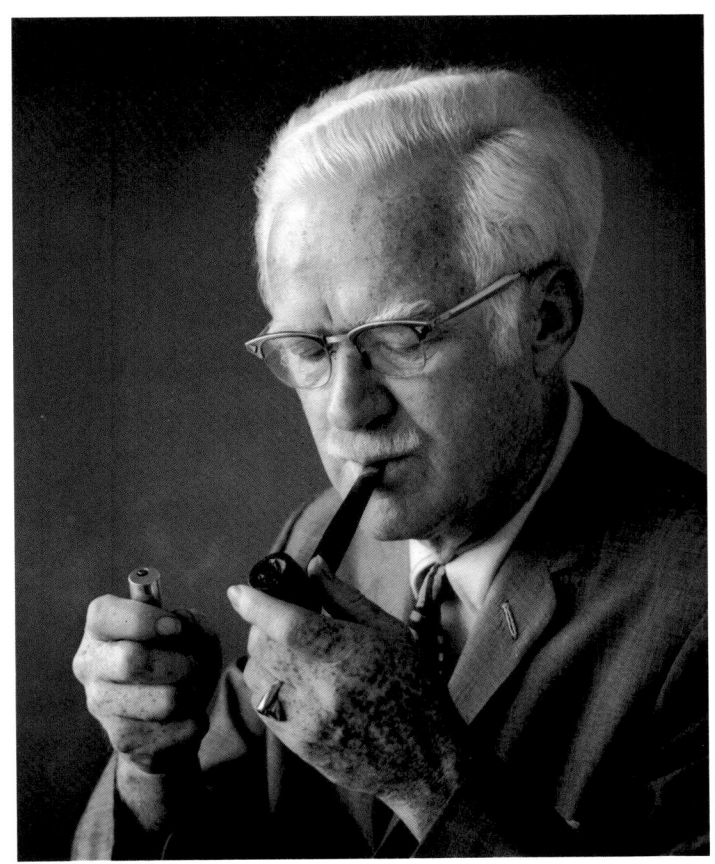

Photograph by Gene Pyle ©

Foreword

Gudmund Vigtel
Director
High Museum of Art
Atlanta

William D. Paul, Jr.
Director
Georgia Museum of Art
Athens

It seems fair to say that the art scene in Georgia was dormant when Lamar Dodd came to Athens in 1937 to guide the Department of Art of The University of Georgia. The art museums in Athens and Columbus did not yet exist, and the High Museum in Atlanta and the museums in Augusta and Savannah were only in their beginnings. It is not surprising that the artistic impetus came from the art schools—especially in Atlanta and Athens—where teachers and facilities could generate activity and interest.

For the many of us who know him so well, it is easy to see how Lamar Dodd fits such a situation to perfection. It was bound to challenge him, and he had the will and spirit to stir things into motion, and the imagination to excite an awareness of art as a source of power and new knowledge. In short, his influence as a teacher—both in the classroom and in the general community of this state—has been crucial to the artistic climate of our region.

It goes without saying that such a contribution has required enormous reserves of discipline and energy. In the light of his pronounced influence, through a major and superbly organized art school, Lamar Dodd's *oeuvre* is very impressive indeed. In spite of the heavy demands of his position, Dodd has managed to produce regularly a long series of works marked by exceptional sensitivity to the world around him. His unhurried, deliberate approach to things is evident in those large, thorough compositions, sparked by a nervous excitement over flickering light, resonant color harmony, and sensuous paint. Especially revealing are his sparse drawings vibrating with life and controlled energy.

To present a review of Lamar Dodd's work as an artist is a major event for us, both on a professional and a personal level. As former students in his classes at the University, the preparations for the exhibition proved to be particularly satisfying to us, and we wish to record here our personal thanks for the artist's gracious collaboration throughout this period. Simultaneously, the aesthetic and historic importance of the exhibition makes this a major study of a principal painter indelibly associated with the arts of Georgia.

The generous scope of this catalogue would not have been possible without the University taking a hand in it, and we wish to express our deep appreciation to President Fred Davison for allowing the book to be published under the auspices of The University of Georgia. We are most grateful to the Dean of University Relations, Louis Griffith, for his work in these arrangements.

It was essential to the usefulness of this catalogue to include a careful study of the artist's work by a knowledgeable writer, and we could not have secured a more respected scholar for this task than Lloyd Goodrich, Advisory Director of the Whitney Museum of American Art. His friendship with the artist made him a particularly qualified critic, and we are extremely grateful to Mr. Goodrich for his thoughtful and sensitive essay.

A great many other individuals have contributed to the success of the exhibition, and we are particularly indebted to Mrs. William Cabin, who compiled all photographic material and the very considerable body of records of Lamar Dodd's career. Dr. Edmund Burke Feldman of the University's art department rendered invaluable service in editing the publication material.

The catalogue was designed most skillfully by Ronald Arnholm, while the majority of the excellent photography reproduced here is the responsibility of two other members of the art department faculty, W. Robert Nix and Wiley D. Sanderson, Jr. To all of these go our admiration and heartfelt thanks.

No large museum exhibition can be carried out without the cooperation of the owners of works of art, and we wish to express our appreciation to the collectors and institutions listed on page 102 for their patient willingness to part with these works for several months. We are especially grateful for assistance given by Erwin S. Barrie, Director of the Grand Central Art Galleries in New York, and Mrs. Colette Roberts, former Director of Grand Central Moderns, who have represented the artist as his dealers over a period of many years.

As a collaborative effort, this exhibition has been most rewarding, and it is with a sense of pride that we present Lamar Dodd's retrospective exhibition to the Georgia public, which owes him so much and which he has served with such inspired dedication.

Introduction

Lloyd Goodrich
Advisory Director
Whitney Museum of
American Art

There are few citizens of the American art world whose activities have covered as wide a range as Lamar Dodd's. Quite aside from his contribution as an artist, he has been an innovating art educator, creator of a major university art department, originator of many projects on behalf of American art, leading figure in national art organizations, and cultural ambassador to other countries.

But with all these activities, Lamar Dodd has always remained primarily an artist. His public accomplishments have been based on his role as a creative painter. In spite of his extra-curricular responsibilities, he has pursued an active artistic career, has produced more than many of his contemporaries, has exhibited widely, and has received many awards and honors.

With all his national and international interests, few artists have been more closely identified with their native grounds. Born and brought up in Georgia, he has been associated with the University of Georgia since he was twenty-eight. After his professional training at the Art Students League of New York he returned to the South, and lived for three years in Birmingham, Alabama. These were Depression times, and he had to make his living by working in an art supply store, painting in his spare time, mostly at night. The art world was dominated by the American scene and regionalist schools, and the rival social protest school. Dodd did not join either camp. His chief subject matter was the local scene, the outskirts of the city—the American landscape in its least idyllic aspects. But there was none of the satire of a Burchfield or the regional patriotism of a Benton. Dodd was not expressing a social viewpoint, either pro or con, but painting the environment he knew best, with as much depth and substance as possible. 'I wanted to create the feeling of solid forms,' he wrote later, 'to capture the mood of a place.' These early landscapes conveyed an intimate feeling for the earth and the manmade features that were part of it: their forms and colors, and above all, the light that fell on them. He also painted some figure subjects, but evidently decided that this was not his métier, for few such works appeared after the 1930s. This has remained true ever since; his subjects have been based primarily on nature and the broad human scene.

In 1936, when he was still in Birmingham, he received a top prize at the Art Institute of Chicago's annual exhibition. Next year he joined the faculty of The University of Georgia, and within a year became head of the art department. At that time the department totalled eight or nine art majors and three teachers, working in the basement of an old house. Today there are over seven hundred art majors, a faculty of fifty-three, and they occupy thirteen buildings, including the Georgia Museum of Art—one of the most extensive and active university art departments in the country. This remarkable growth is due largely to Lamar Dodd's creative imagination, energy and administrative ability.

From the late 1940s Dodd spent his short summer vacations on the island of Monhegan, ten miles off the Maine coast. With its rocky cliffs rising sheer out of deep water, receiving the full force of Atlantic storms, Monhegan was rich in pictorial drama. His Monhegan seascapes began a new phase in Dodd's art. The elemental battle between sea and shore, the white fury of waves breaking against black rocks, fascinated and challenged him. He has told how, inspired by this new subject matter, he at first tried to include everything he saw and felt; but 'later I realized I was trying to put in everything at once . . . I had to select, to make a choice, to say something—not everything.' He selected, he simplified, he concentrated on essentials. These marines showed a fresh realization of nature's dynamic energy, a quality that had not been apparent in his quiet inland landscapes. There was a new sense of movement: the thrust and counterthrust of massive rock forms, the opposing force of breaking waves. The prevailing mood was stormy and somber. The color was deep and dark: black rocks, gray-blue sea, white foam, threatening sky. These seascapes marked a step away from naturalistic representation toward a new selectivity and a more conscious sense of design.

Many of them were actually painted in his studio back home, from memories and sketches of Monhegan. At least one had an unusual genesis. After *The Breaker* won a prize in 1946, he was asked where he had painted it, and replied, 'In my studio in Athens, Georgia, *from a still life*.' He had been working on a still life and had turned it upside-down to study the composition, and found that it suggested a wave breaking on rocks; so he took another canvas, adopted the inverted design, and painted his prize-winner. Design was becoming as important as subject matter.

By this time his style had developed certain characteristics that were to mark it thenceforth. First and most fundamental, it revealed him as a natural painter, with a sensuous love of pigment and its handling, and of translating nature's forms and colors into the physical richness of the painted surface. This painterly gift had appeared in his early landscapes and particularly in his still lifes, in which the physical qualities of objects were the central motif. It was strengthened and enriched in his seascapes with their broad, free brushwork. As he developed, this painterliness was to take on added skill and refinement, with no loss of the basic pleasure in handling paint.

Another marked characteristic was his graphic sense. His style was founded on drawing —on clear, controlled drawing with the brush. Often, as in *Ashen Gods* and *Sentinels*, two paintings of dead trees on Monhegan, the forms were defined by strong black outlines, drawn with skill and energy. This fundamental graphic sense was to continue throughout the changing phases of his later work, gaining constantly in control and precision.

From the first, Dodd had shown himself to be a born colorist, with that harmonic sense that cannot be taught but must be innate. His Monhegan seascapes had been in a deliberately restricted chromatic range, somewhat dark, with few brilliant notes, but with a fine use of subtly varied grays. This command of limited but skillfully related tones indicated that he was capable of a much wider range of color harmonies in the future.

Through the 1940s Dodd's artistic language remained basically naturalistic, but revealing a growing awareness of the essential element of design. At first this was most evident in his still lifes, where subject matter was subordinate to visual factors. His design sense was still more instinctive than theoretical; although a teacher he placed no emphasis on traditional concepts of design. His was a personal style, working out compositional problems in a pragmatic way. In his Monhegan paintings natural forms were used with increasing freedom and a more conscious striving for design. This trend toward planned design grew during the late 1940s and early 1950s. *Of the Sea* (1951), for example, combined representation with an obviously thought-out pattern of more or less flat angular receding planes, superimposed and overlapping—a concept suggestive of Oriental art. This was a basic type of design that he was to use frequently thenceforth, with increasing complexity and command.

Dodd made his first visit to Europe in the fall of 1953, when he was forty-four, an unusually mature age. This stay lasted about a year, on a grant from the General Education Board of the Rockefeller Foundation to study procedures in art education. But he also found time to see cities and countries, to visit museums, to paint, and to make sketches and notes for future paintings. (Also, characteristically, to take about 6,000 color photographs for his University art-history colleagues.) This first European tour was followed by several more in the next few years, usually on assignments from governmental agencies. As he wrote in 1961, 'I have always sustained a firm belief in the progress of understanding, between peoples of the world, through educational and cultural exchanges. This belief has been intensified in the past decade as I have travelled around the world, both on personal trips devoted to study and observation, and on cultural exchange missions.' In 1956 his travels extended beyond Europe to Turkey and the Near East; then in 1958/9 to Belgium, Russia, India, Thailand, Korea, Japan and the Philippines, for the State Department's Advisory Committee on the Arts.

These travels had a decisive effect on his own art. Not that he attempted to paint on-thespot travelogues. All or most of his foreign-inspired subjects were painted after his return, from memories, sketches, notes, and sometimes his photographs used as reminders. But the experience of seeing the ancient cities and landscape of Europe and Asia liberated his art in every respect— in color, in freedom of handling, in design. The lingering traces of naturalistic detail were eliminated. The forms of nature were translated into the forms of art. The soaring lines of cathedrals were transformed into semi-abstract designs of vertical lines and successive rising planes, precise and finely related. In his compositions of Italian hill towns the houses climbing the hillsides formed complex structures of receding planes. A fleet of Venetian gondolas at rest, with their bold prows and curving lines, became an intricate interlaced linear pattern. In these new works the element of pure design, freed from unfunctional naturalism, had become fully conscious, and more completely realized.

A corresponding expansion took place in his color. A particular revelation was the color of Venice—gold, orange, terracotta, contrasting with the deep blue, violet and blue-green of the lagoons. His earlier grays gave way to colors of a new strength, variety and depth— positive hues in direct juxtaposition. When he did revert to a restricted range, his grays had an added refinement and subtlety. With each new visual experience his range widened; the multi-colored crowds and scenes of the Near East and Asia brought an increasing brilliance and gaiety to his palette.

In this evolution there was a growing trend toward abstraction, toward using nature as a springboard for free creation in form, color and line. But only occasionally has Dodd practised pure abstraction. For him the visible world remains the ultimate source of art. Almost all his paintings have originated in visual reality, no matter how far they may depart from it. In this he differed from the dominant abstract-expressionist school of the 1940s and 1950s. And also in his belief in conscious control of the language of art, and his disbelief in the virtue of action painting, in which the act of manipulating the pigment had much to do with determining the forms. Even his most abstract works are governed by conscious design. 'At times today we frequently hear a painter state that when he starts a canvas he has no idea of what he is going to do,' he wrote in 1964. 'I seriously doubt the validity of that statement, if we are expected to accept it per se . . . If we can honestly trace the origin of some of our abstract expressionist paintings that appear to show so little concern with the visual world, we might discover that often this origin was based on some astute perception of even a fragmentary portion of life.'

On the other hand, his work does not belong to the purist geometrical school with its total non-objectivity and complete planning. 'I do not believe that any painter can visualize completely his finished product as he faces a bare canvas, any more than the scientist can predict his discoveries before the experiment takes place,' he wrote in 1951.

With his convictions about the social value of art, Dodd believes that painting is a way of communication, but he sees no conflict between this and abstraction. 'The public frequently looks at an abstraction and remarks, the painting has nothing to say,' he has written. 'I believe that art should be a form of communication, but no form of communication can operate unless there are two parties—one sending, the other receiving . . . We must bring something to the work of art in order to receive something in return.'

Even in his paintings nearest to abstraction, his style is still basically graphic; the forms are drawn clearly and precisely, with a fine sensitive touch. For him, good craftsmanship is a virtue in itself. To prospective jurors he suggested the questions: 'Does the painting show evidence of intelligent discipline? Is the craftsmanship sound? Has the painter mastered his tools and techniques? Does he respect his materials? As is true in many fields, uncontrolled skill is a liability; controlled skill is an asset.'

The development of Dodd's art has been one of steady growth. 'One's study is never finished,' he wrote in 1964, 'and I, as a painter, will remain a student for my entire life . . . The process of change, the hoped-for growth, add joy to the act of painting because, without the continuing quest for knowledge and increased vision and greater comprehension, painting can become a deadly vacuum, a routine of assembly-line-like production.' But his evolution has remained singularly consistent; there has never been any abrupt reversal, any complete abandonment of earlier views. The more abstract works have grown out of the more representational, and are directly related to them.

This is true even of his most advanced recent work, devoted to the theme of the exploration of space. In 1963 he was one of seven painters invited by the National Aeronautics and Space Administration to record the manned orbital flight of Astronaut Gordon Cooper. The NASA project was a recognition of the fact that no matter how accurate the camera may be, it still misses some essential truths that only the artist's pencil and brush can capture. There was precedent for this project in the 19th-century artists who accompanied the Western explorations, the pictorial reporters of the Civil War, the painters commissioned by the War Department in World Wars I and II, and the more recent Air Force art program. But in the words of Lester Cooke of the National Gallery, 'NASA has a significant advantage in that the programmers can pinpoint the time and place where history will be made, with a minimum margin of error, and offer the artist a ringside seat.'

Dodd and his colleagues were given the opportunity for five days to roam the installations on Cape Canaveral and sketch them. Then they shared the almost-unbearable suspense of the countdown, and the final earth-shattering flame and roar of the liftoff. From their sketches the seven artists produced paintings which joined NASA's growing collection of works devoted to the exploration of space.

It was natural that Dodd would again be invited to help record the Apollo 11 moon mission in July 1969. This time almost fifty artists participated: some at the Cape (re-named Cape Kennedy), some at the control room in Houston, some on the recovery carrier *Hornet* in the Pacific. Dodd witnessed the launching at the Cape; then to Houston, where he watched the whole journey to and from the moon. On returning to Athens he worked at white heat for two months, painting many hours every day, and producing no fewer than twenty-five paintings, including some of the largest and most complex that he had ever made.

Dodd was especially qualified to picture this historic event. He has the intellectual curiosity, the sense of history, the broad human concern. As a painter he has always been interested in space and motion. His space paintings are no mere factual records, but an imaginative, poetic interpretation of man's first landing on another planet, embodied in a style the freest and boldest of his entire career. In these paintings, each so different in imagery, we are given a vivid, penetrating sense of the immense loneliness of outer space, the fathomless darkness of the universe, the burning effulgence of the sun, the smallness and yet the radiance of our earth as seen from enormous distances. We feel the fantastic speed of the spacecraft hurtling through the dark universe; we even have the sensation of weightlessness. The strange shapes of the sunlit sides of the moon and the earth are translated into visionary forms and colors entirely new in the artist's work. In this series Lamar Dodd has crowned his long creative career with his most original and impressive works.

Plates

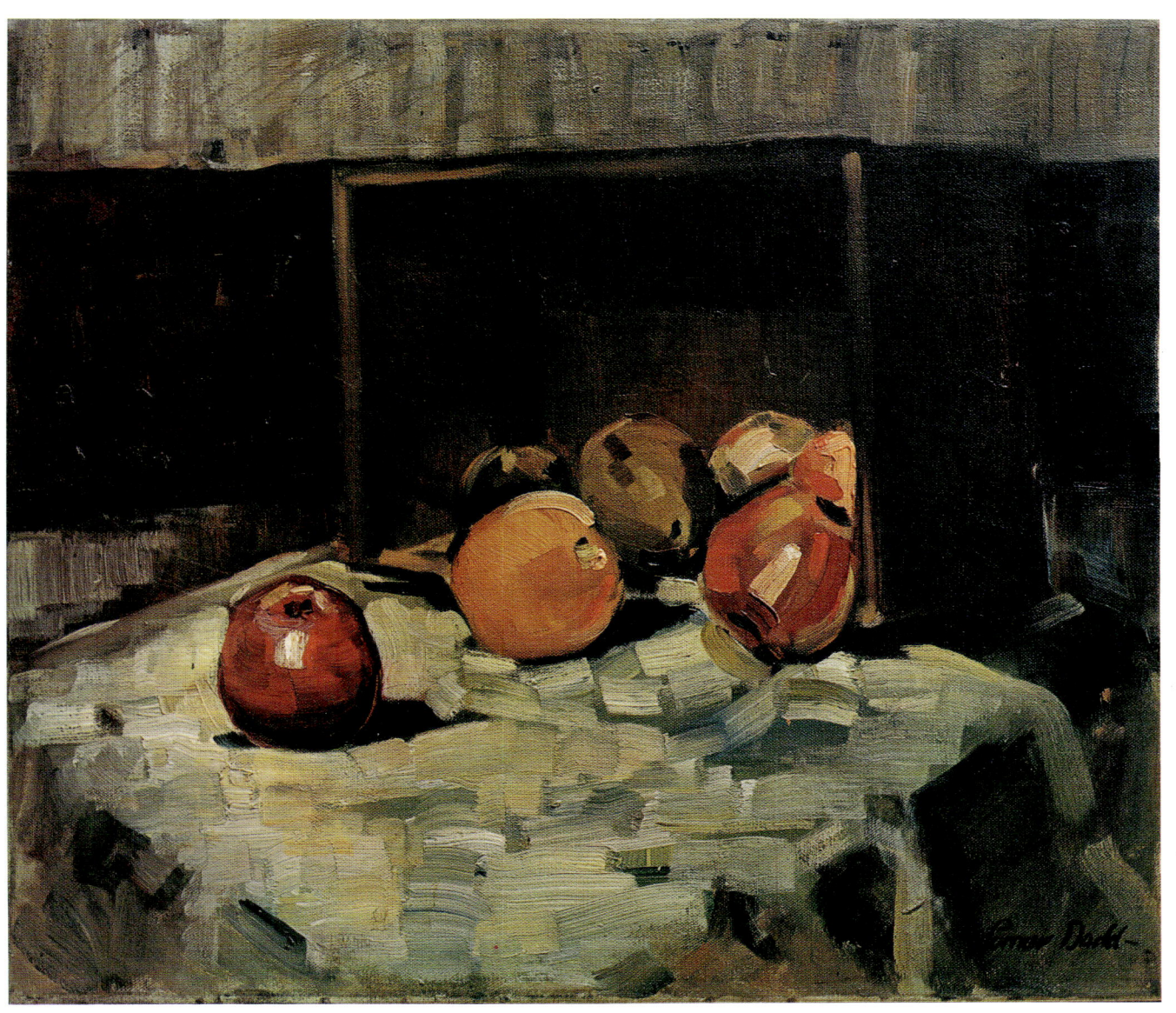

9. The Yellow Skirt

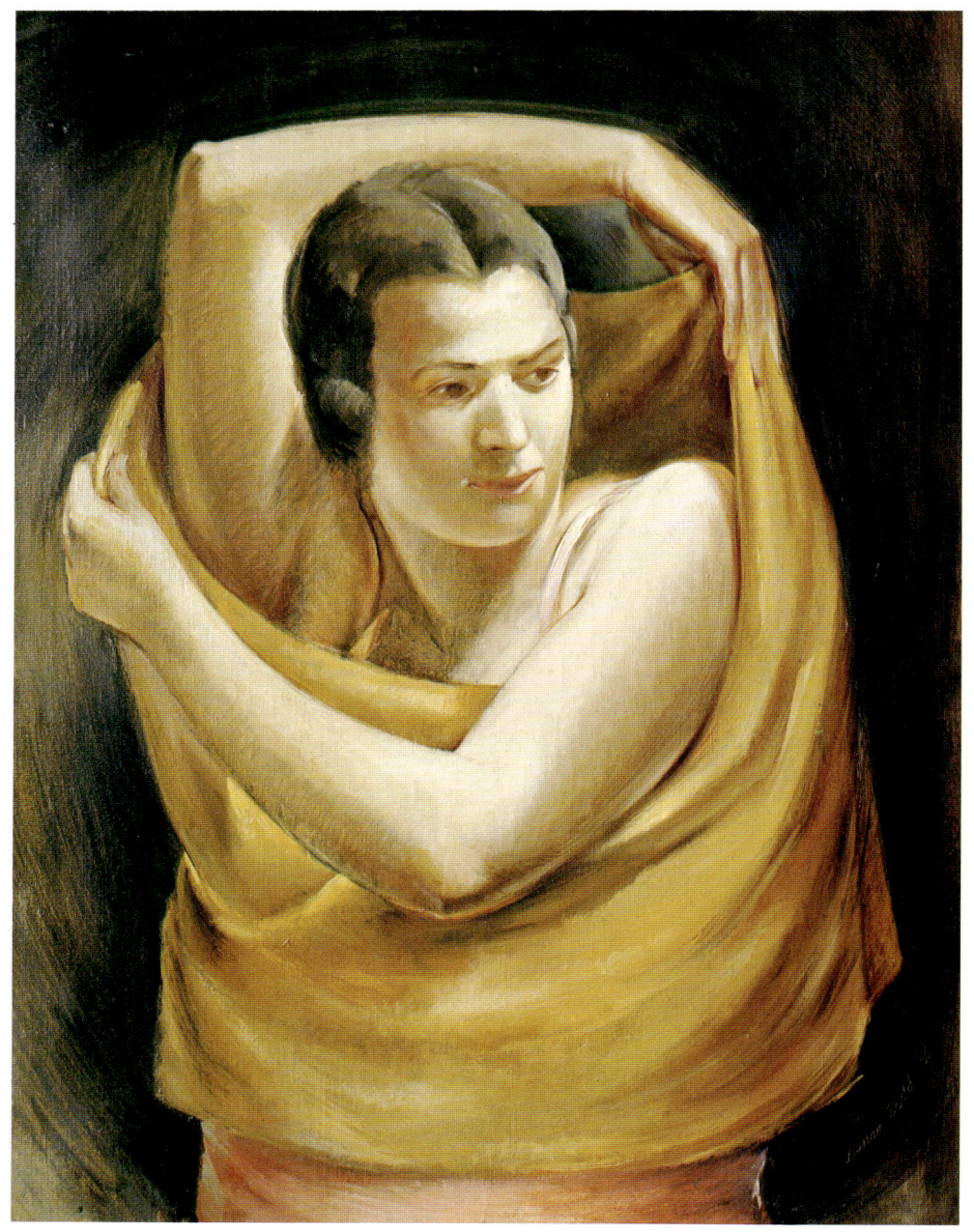

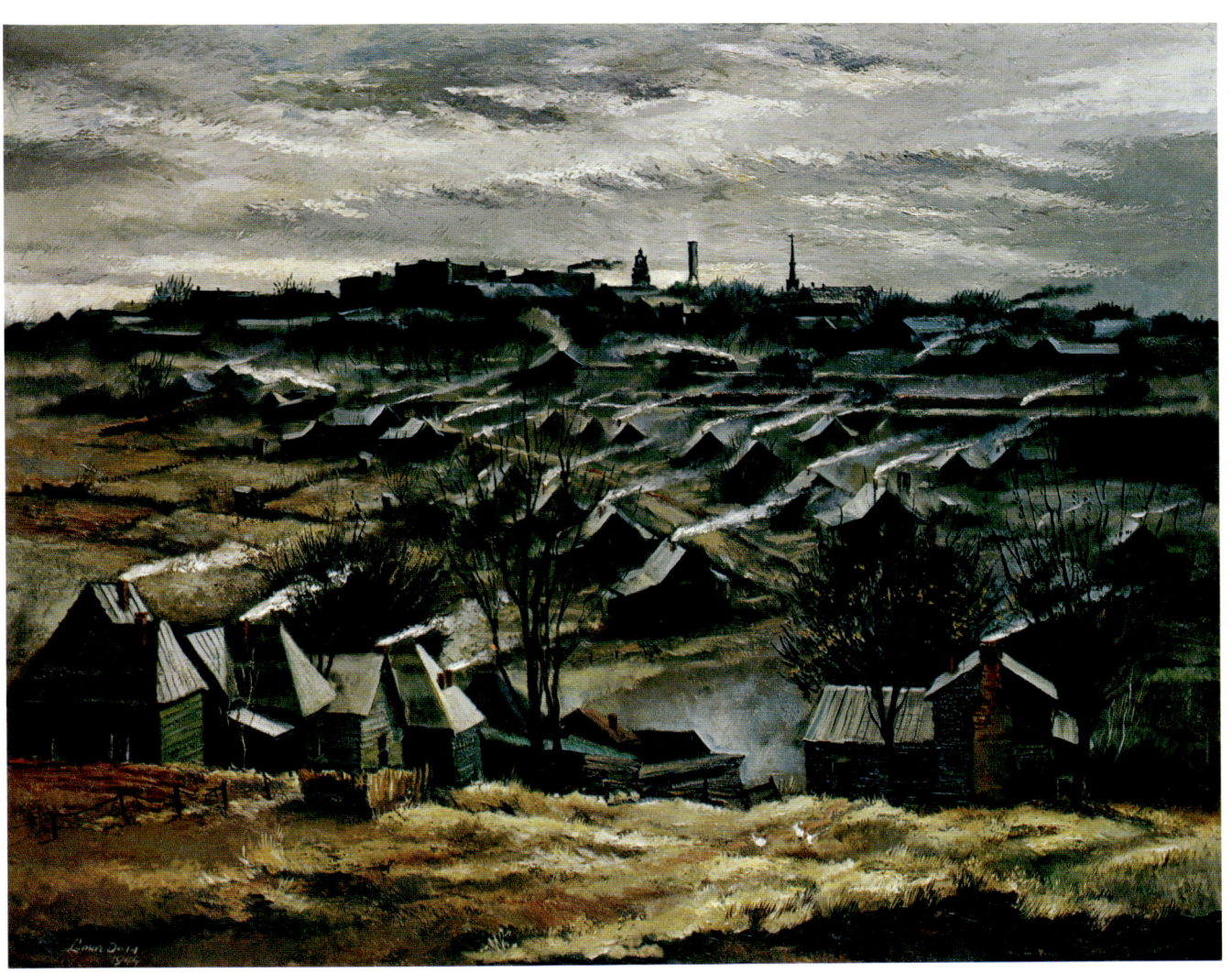

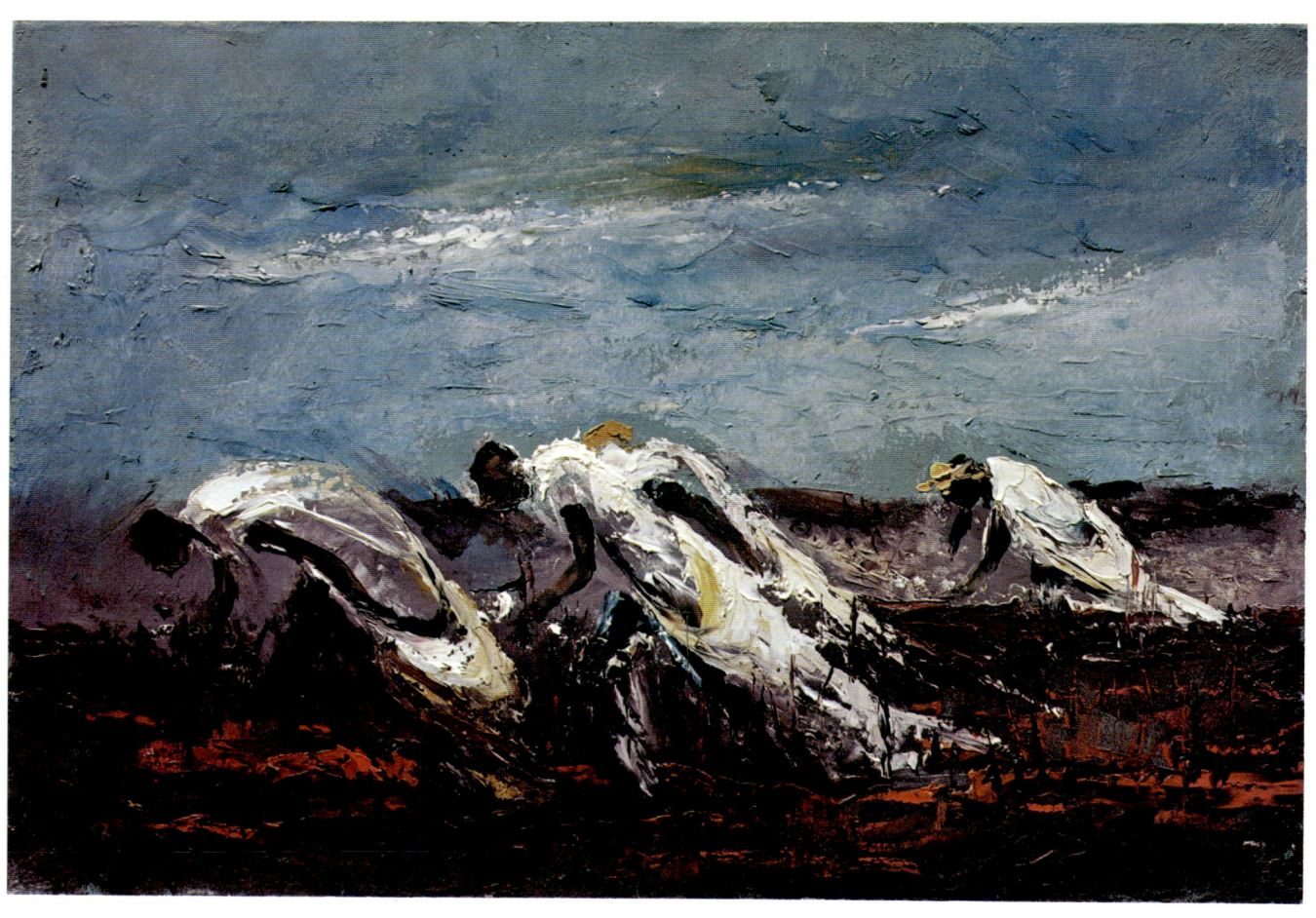

Cotton Pickers

1. Manhattan Bridge, Bowery

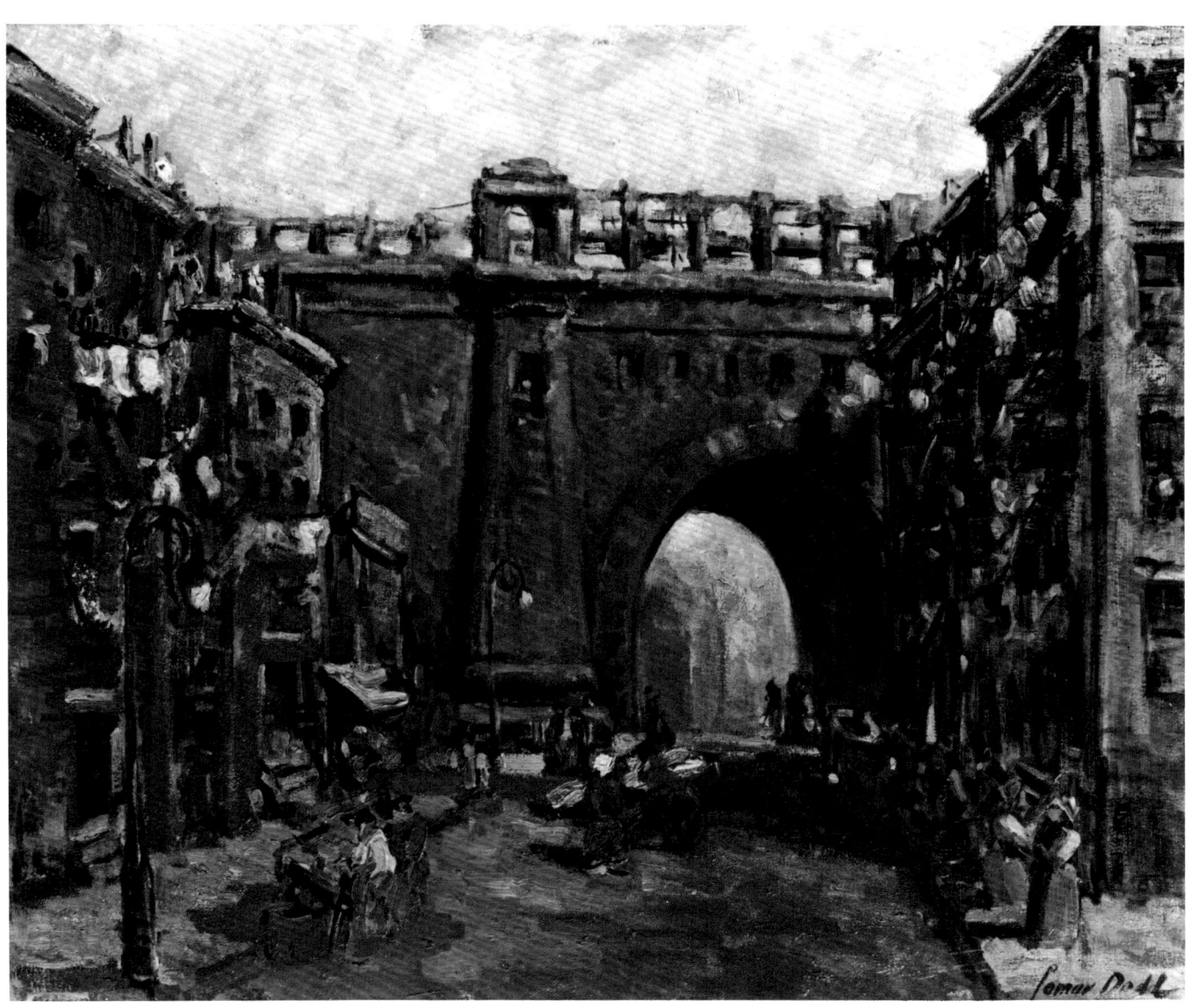

3. Excavation for Empire State Building

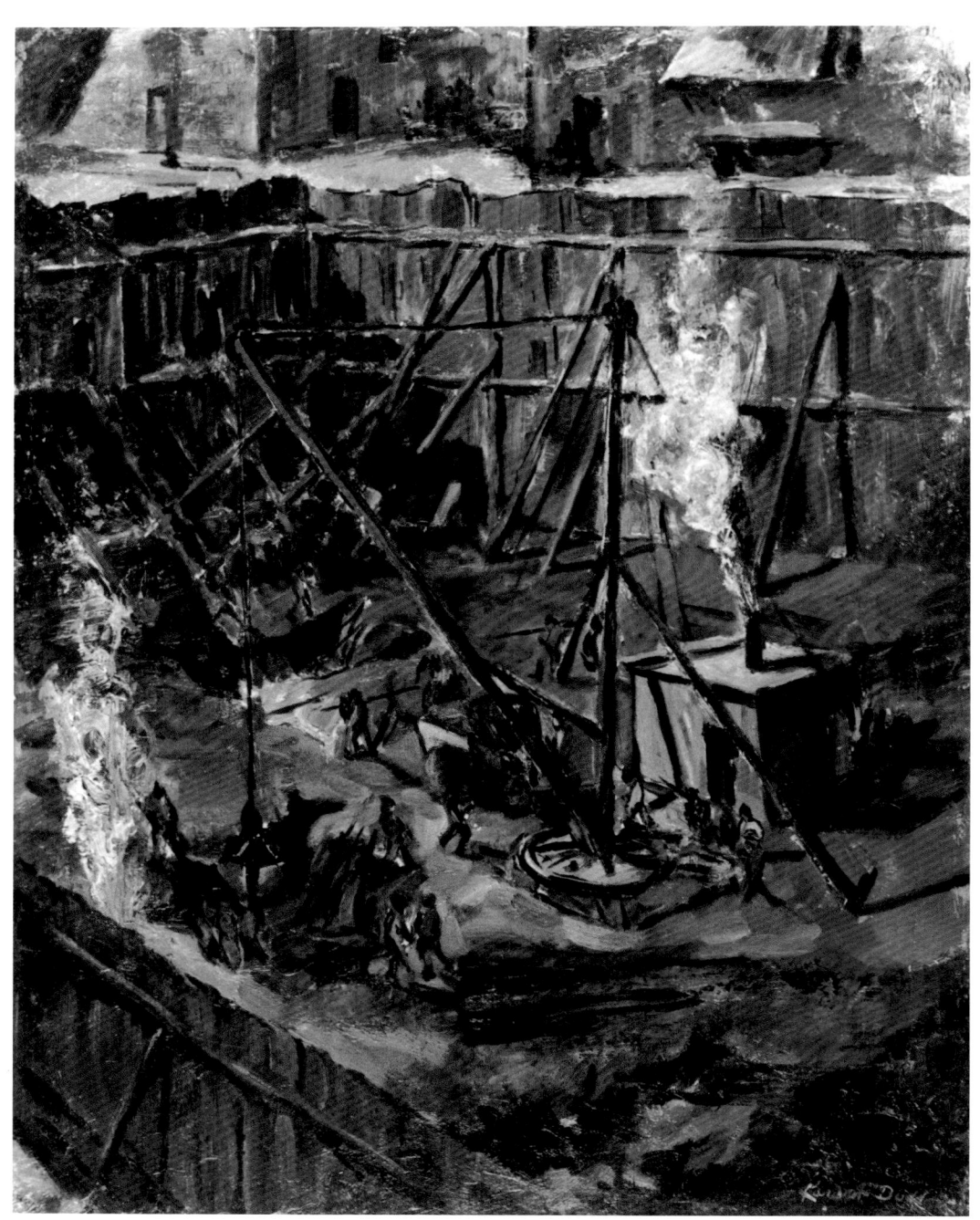

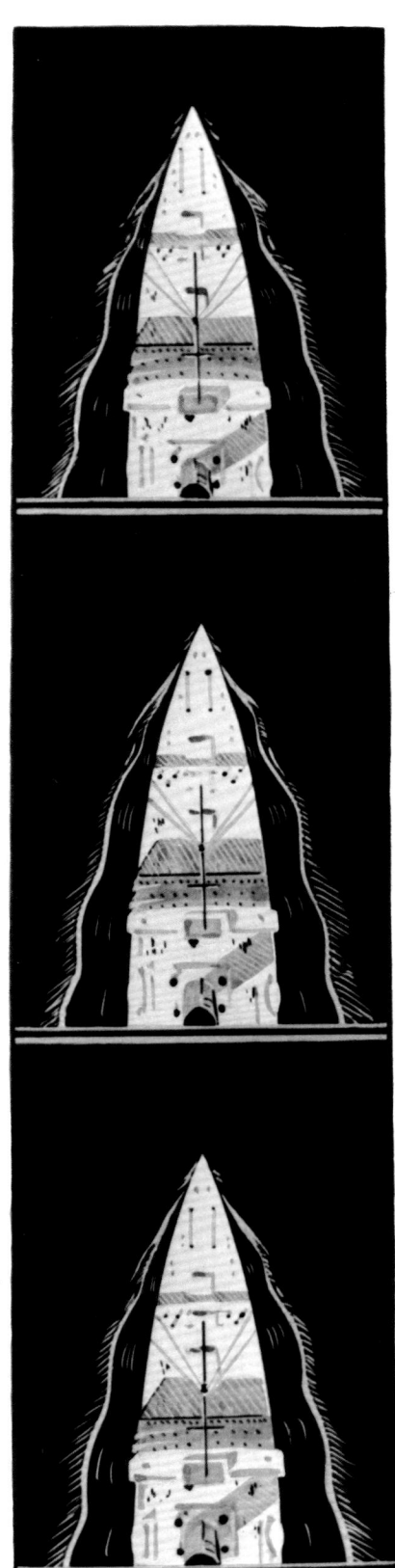

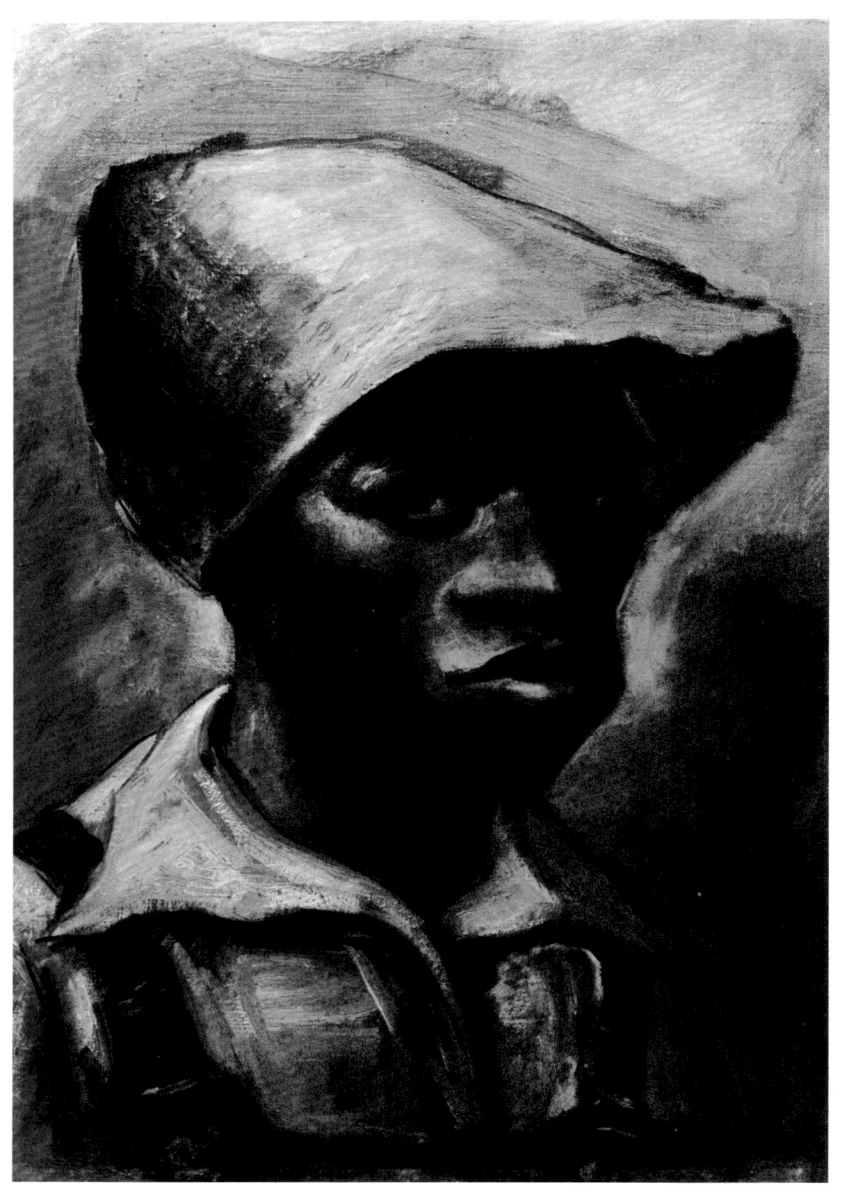

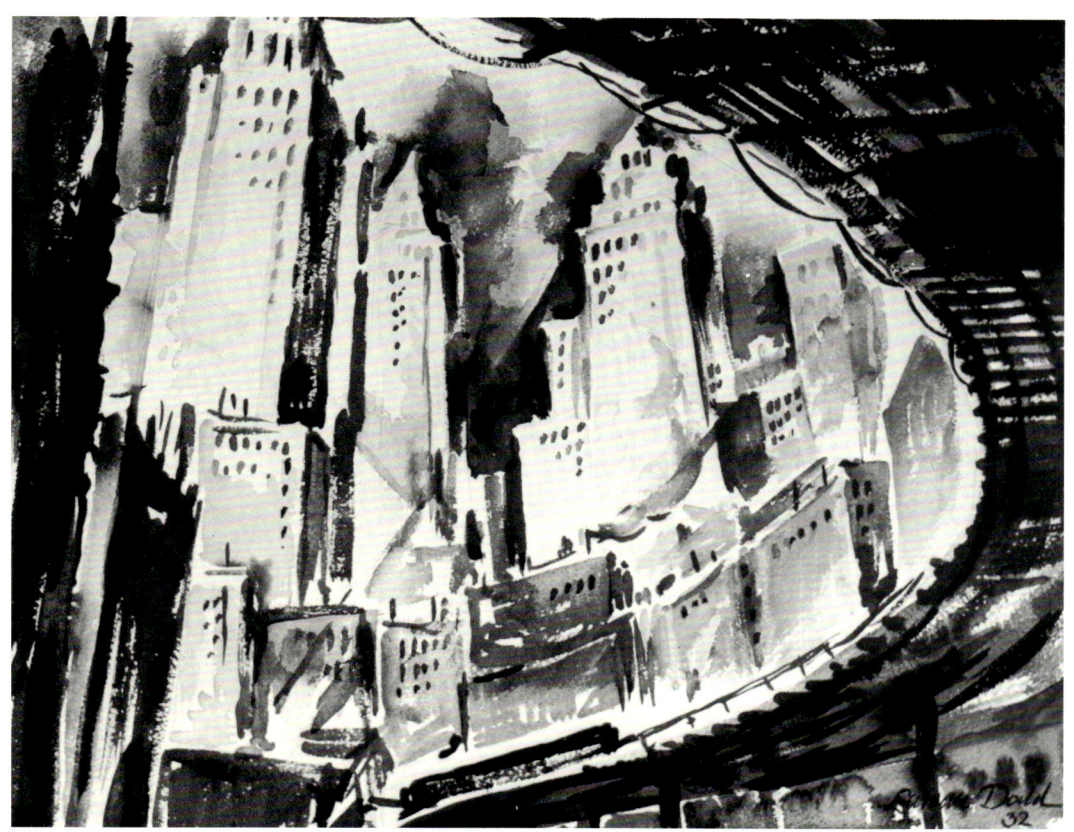

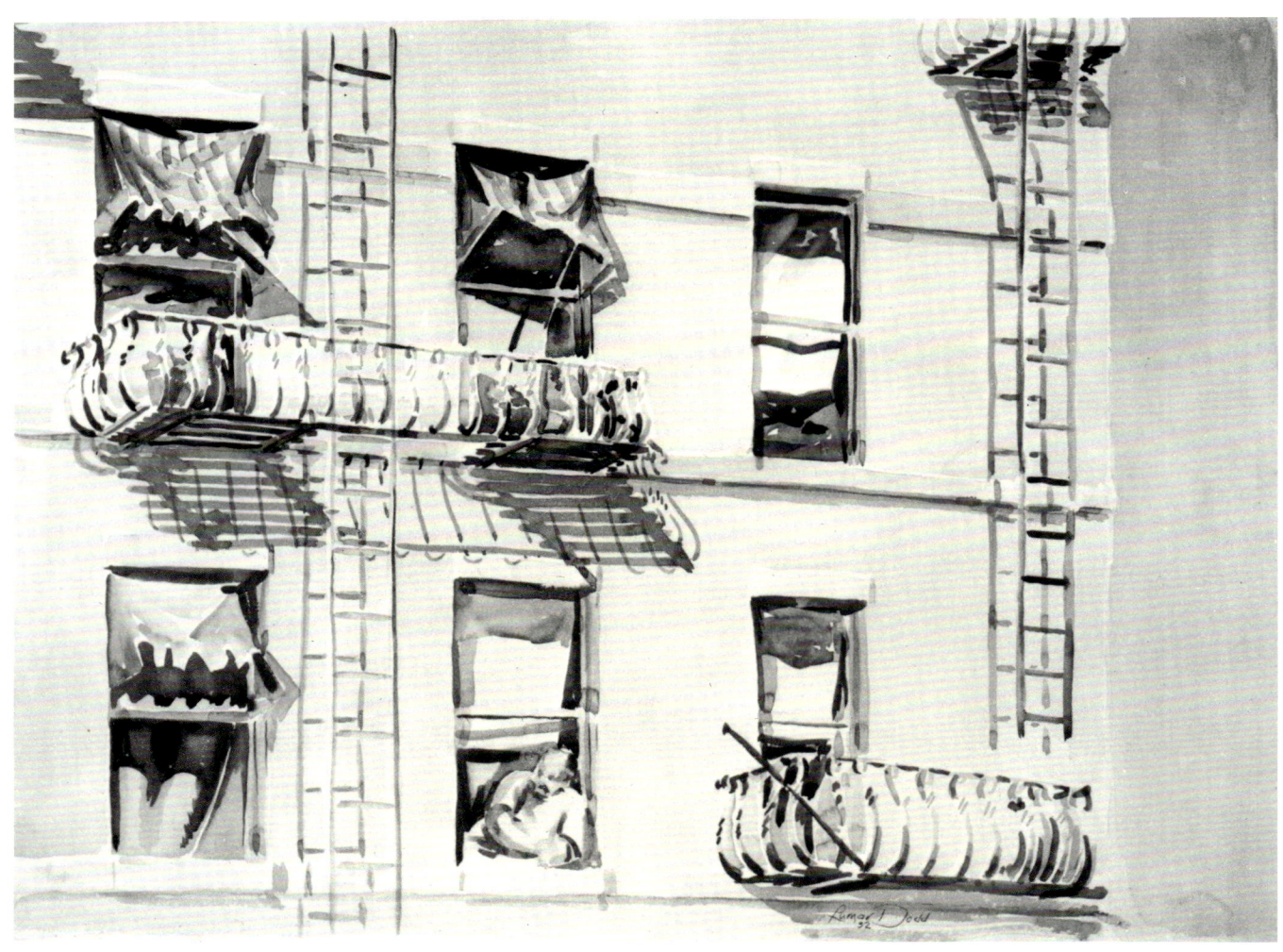

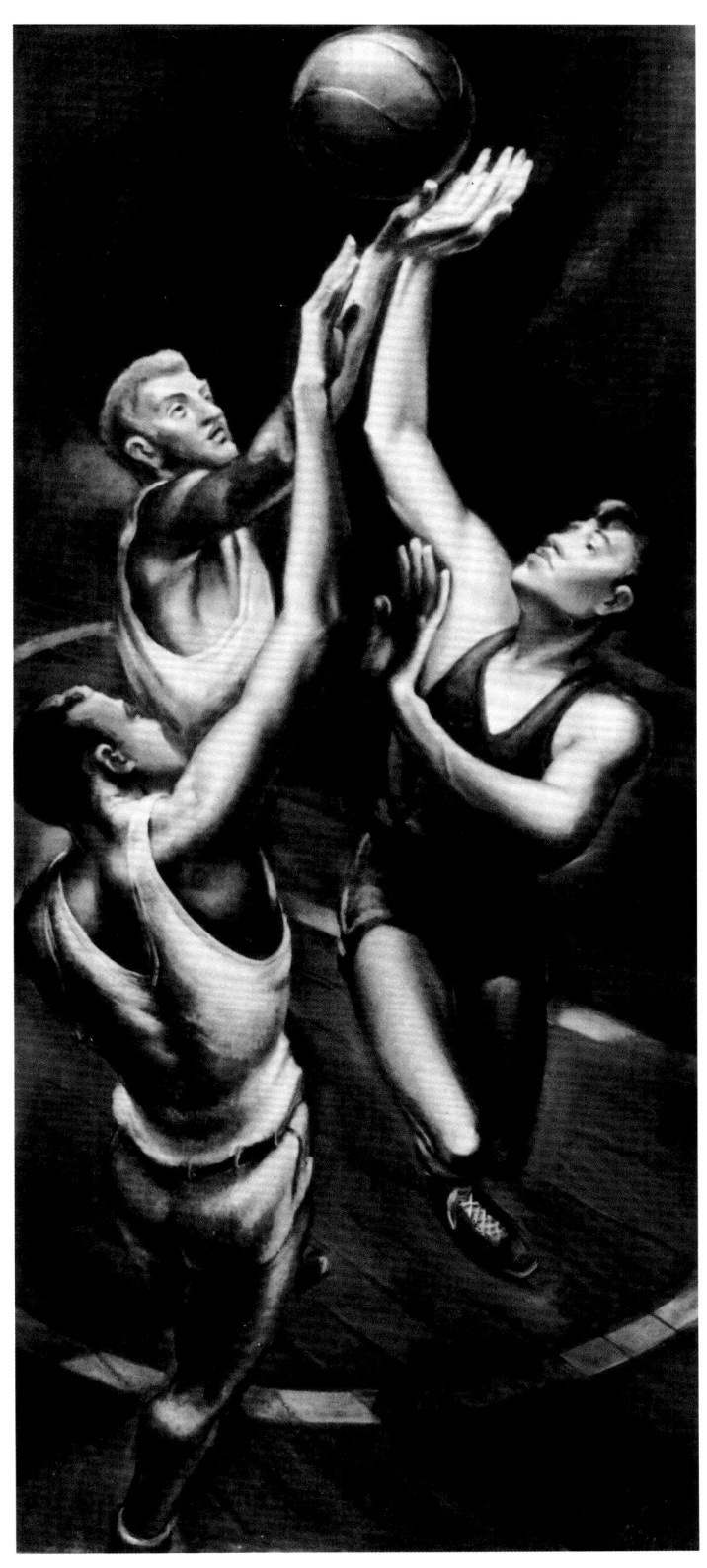

Basketball

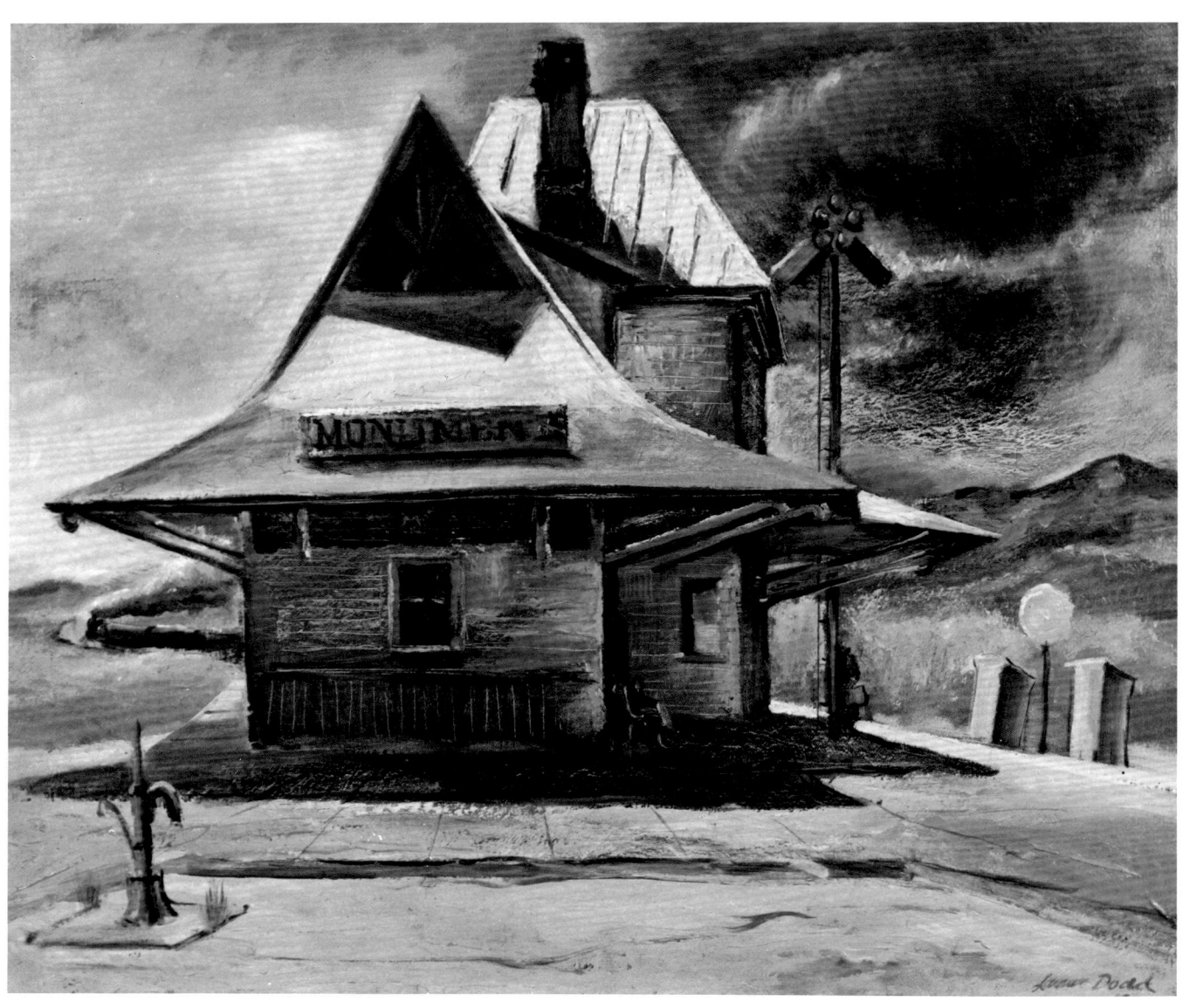

12. A Rainy Ride

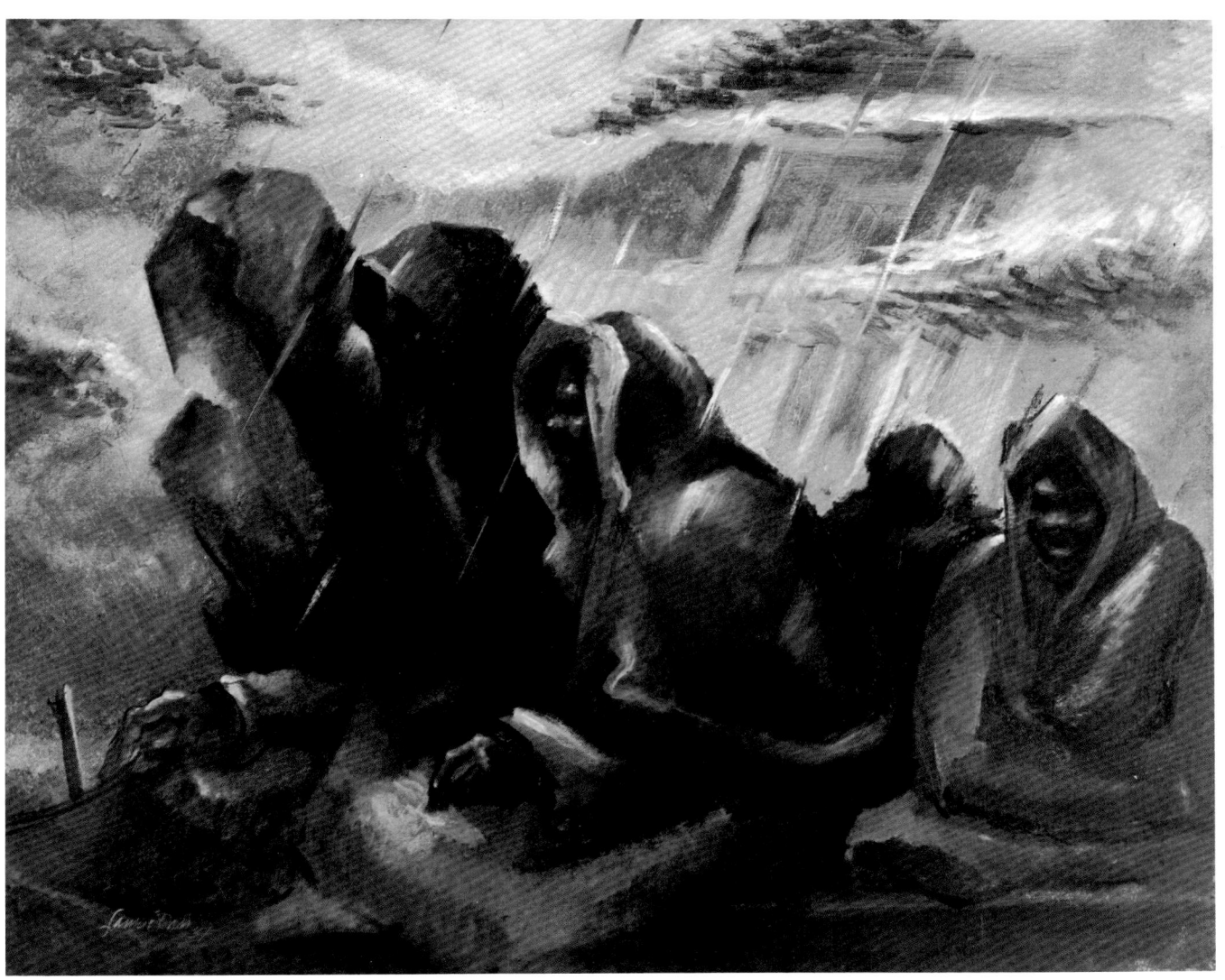

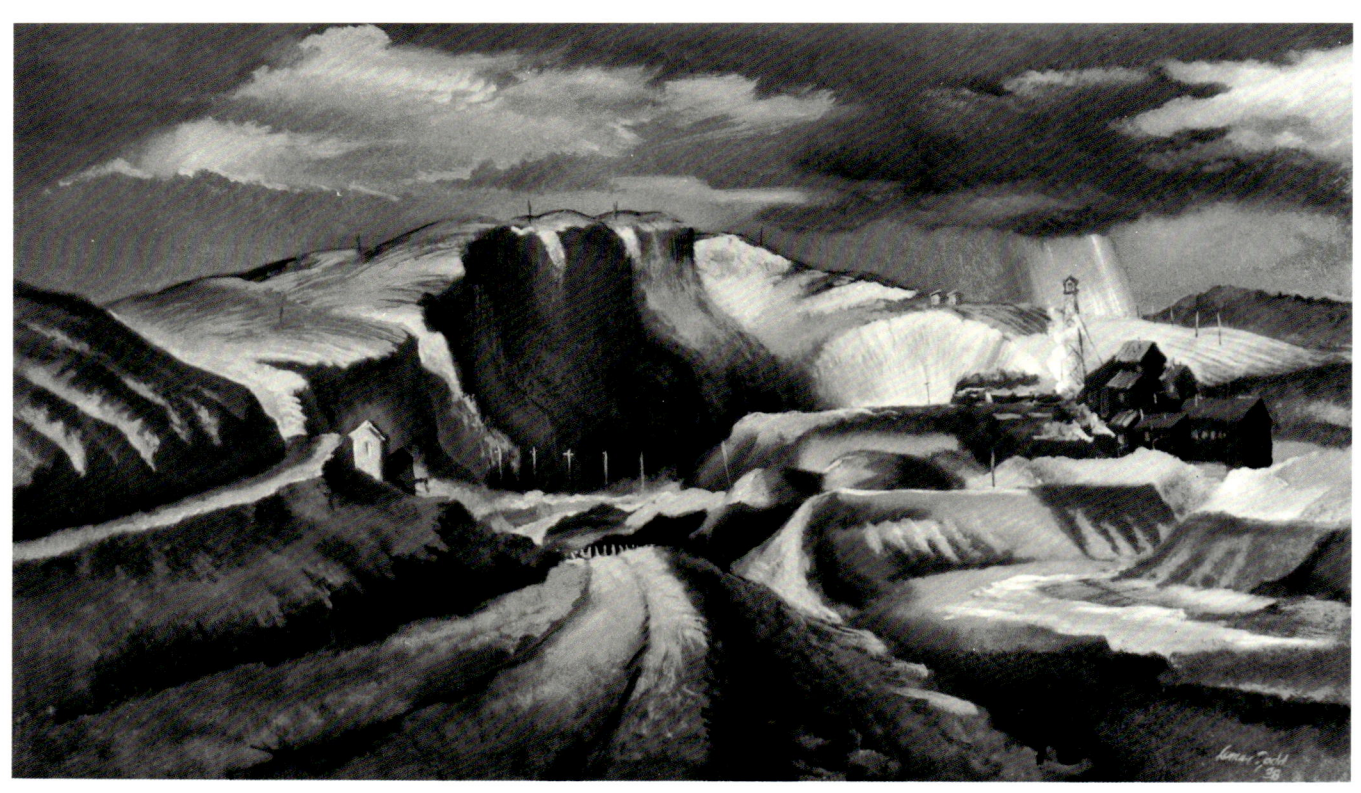

Copperhill

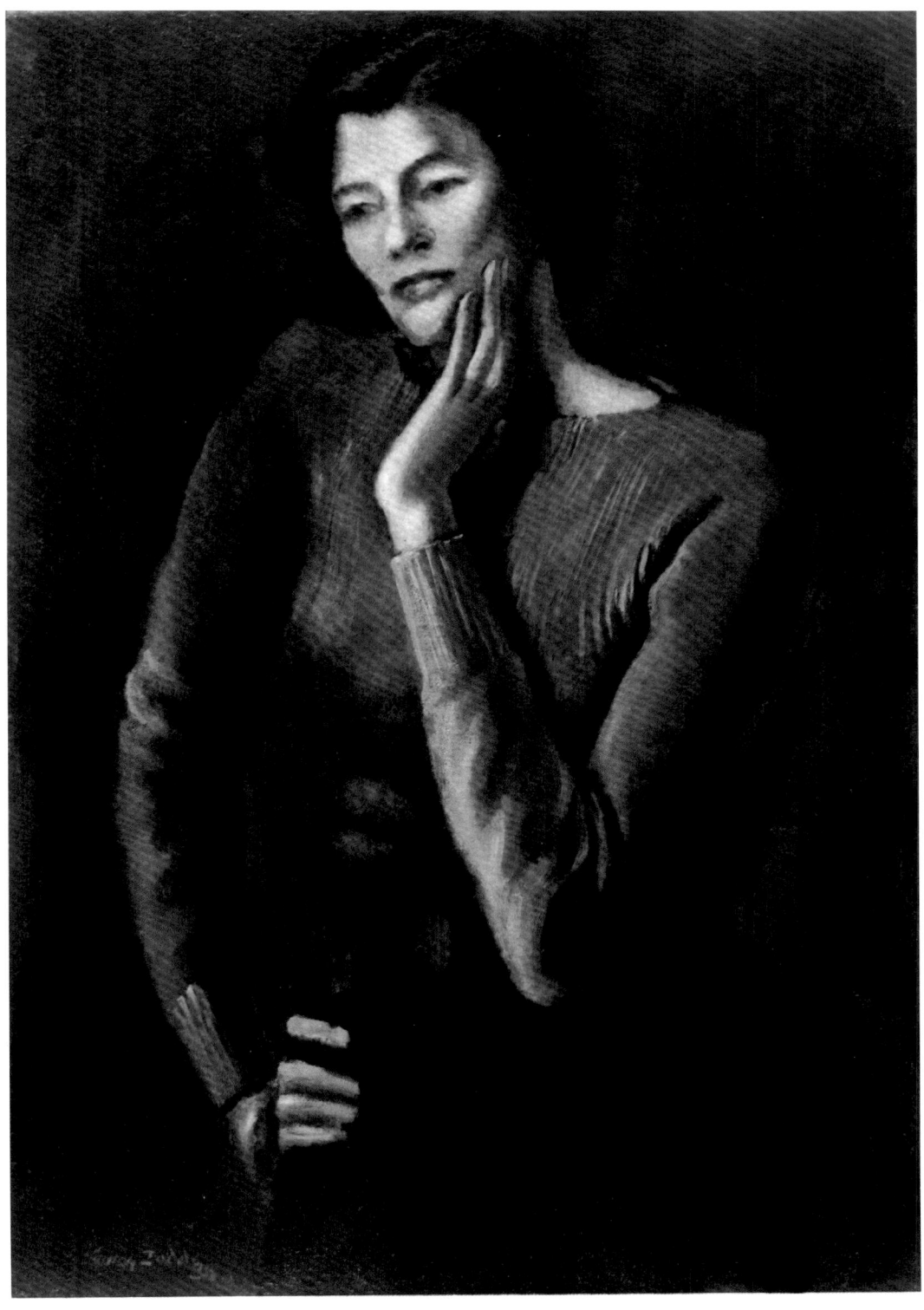

Rella

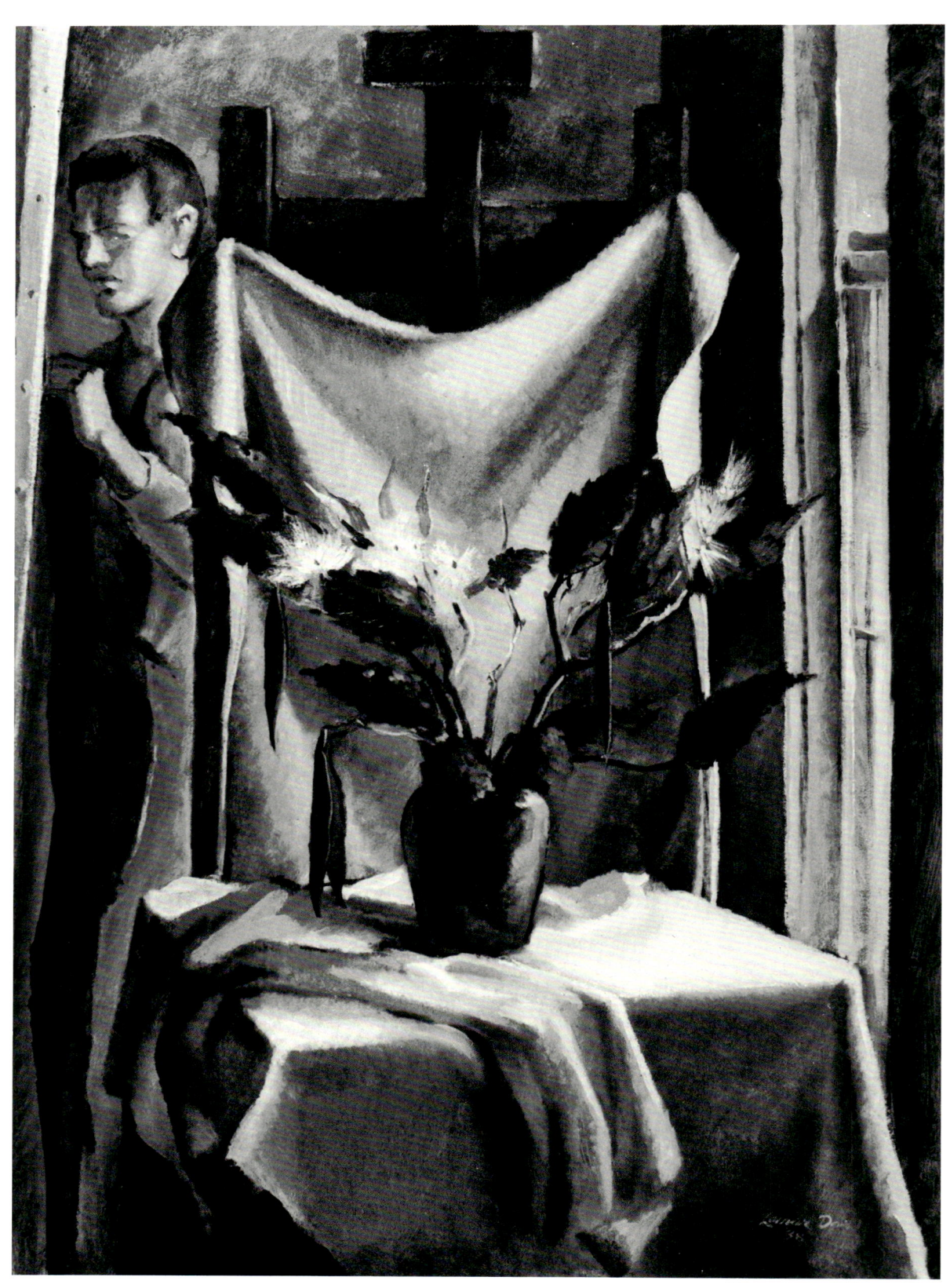

17. View of Athens

Lent by Dr. and Mrs. Fred C. Davison

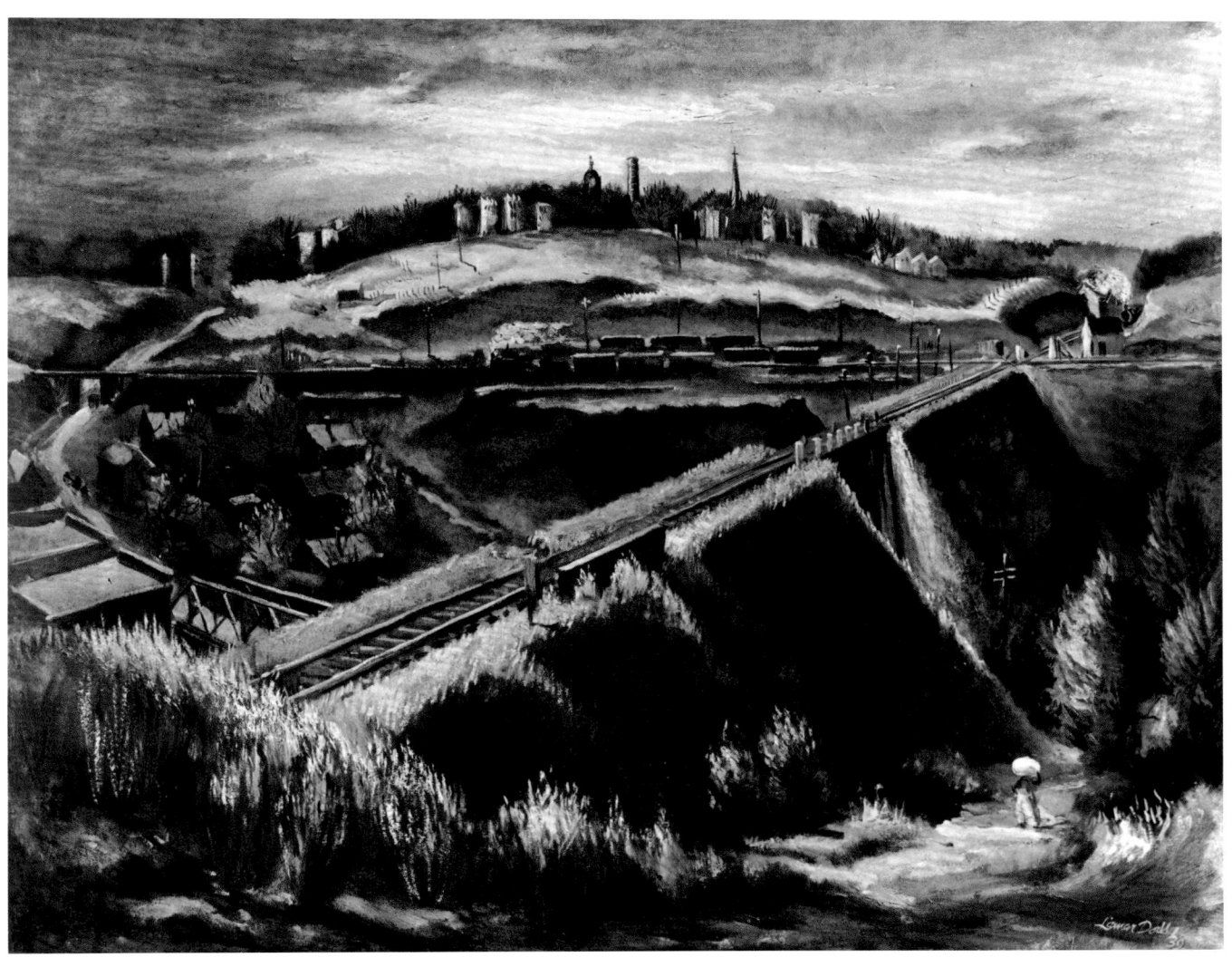

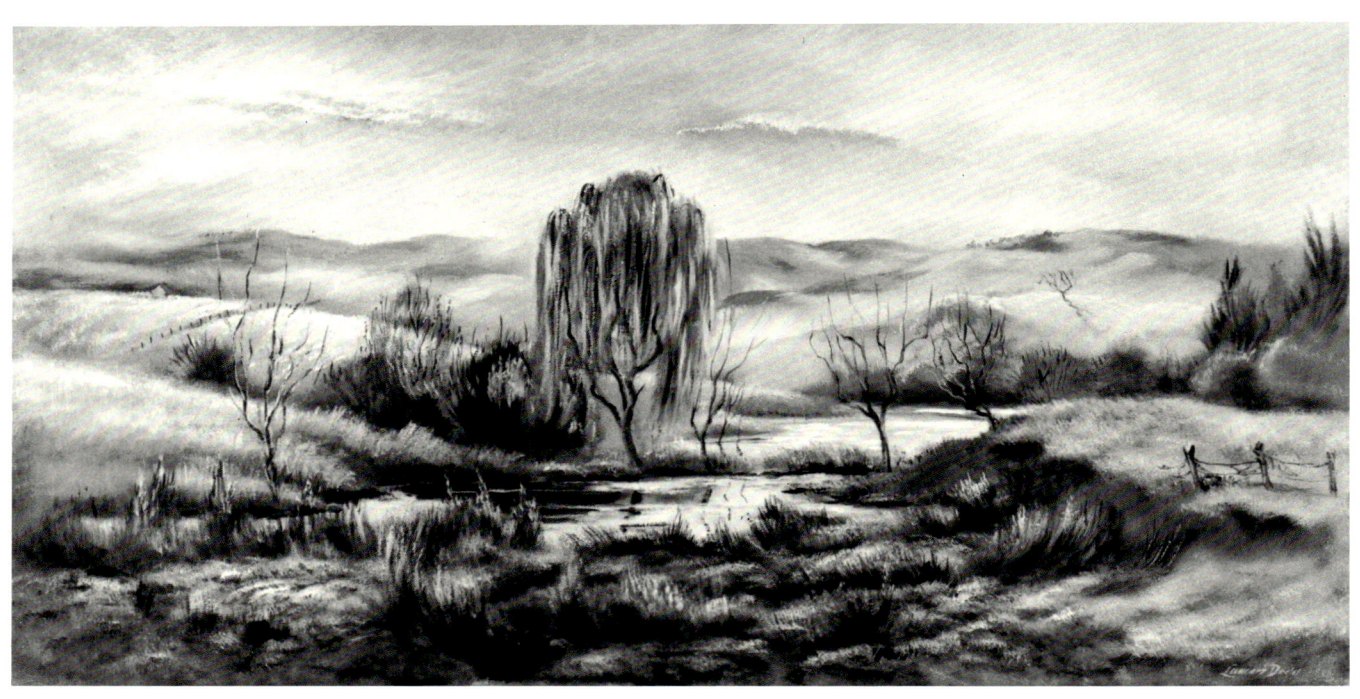

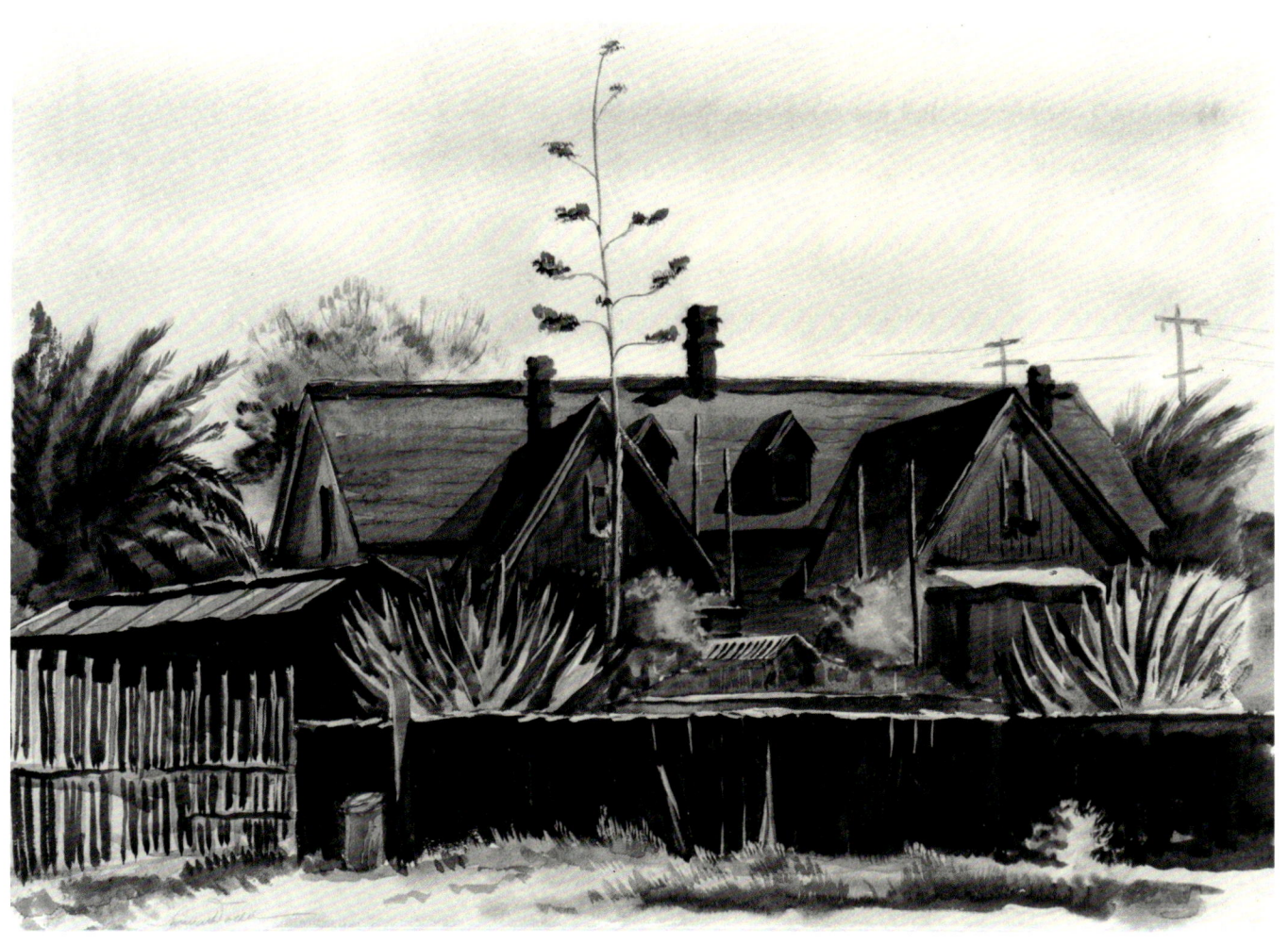

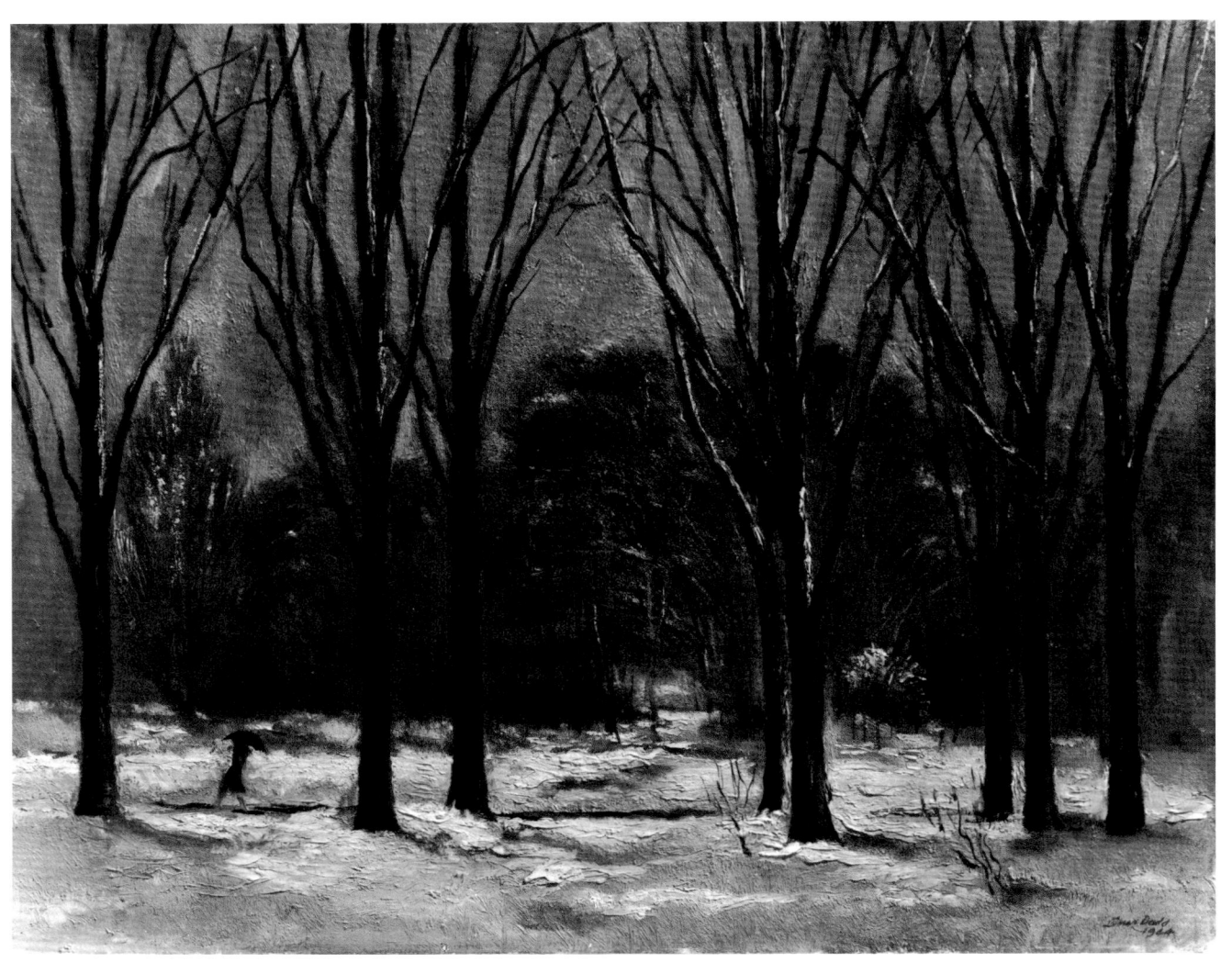

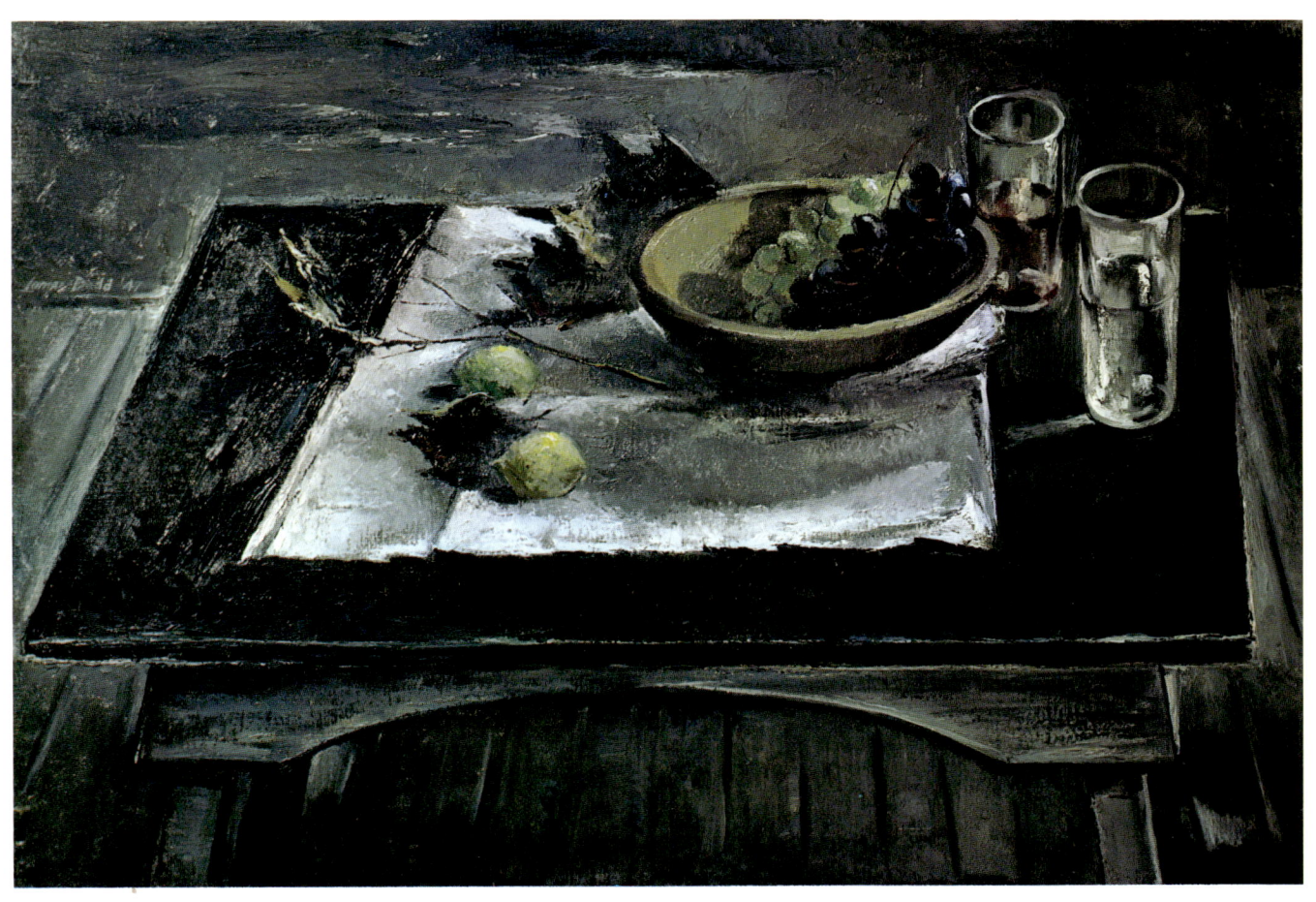

34. Cascade

Lent by the Georgia Museum of Art, The University of Georgia

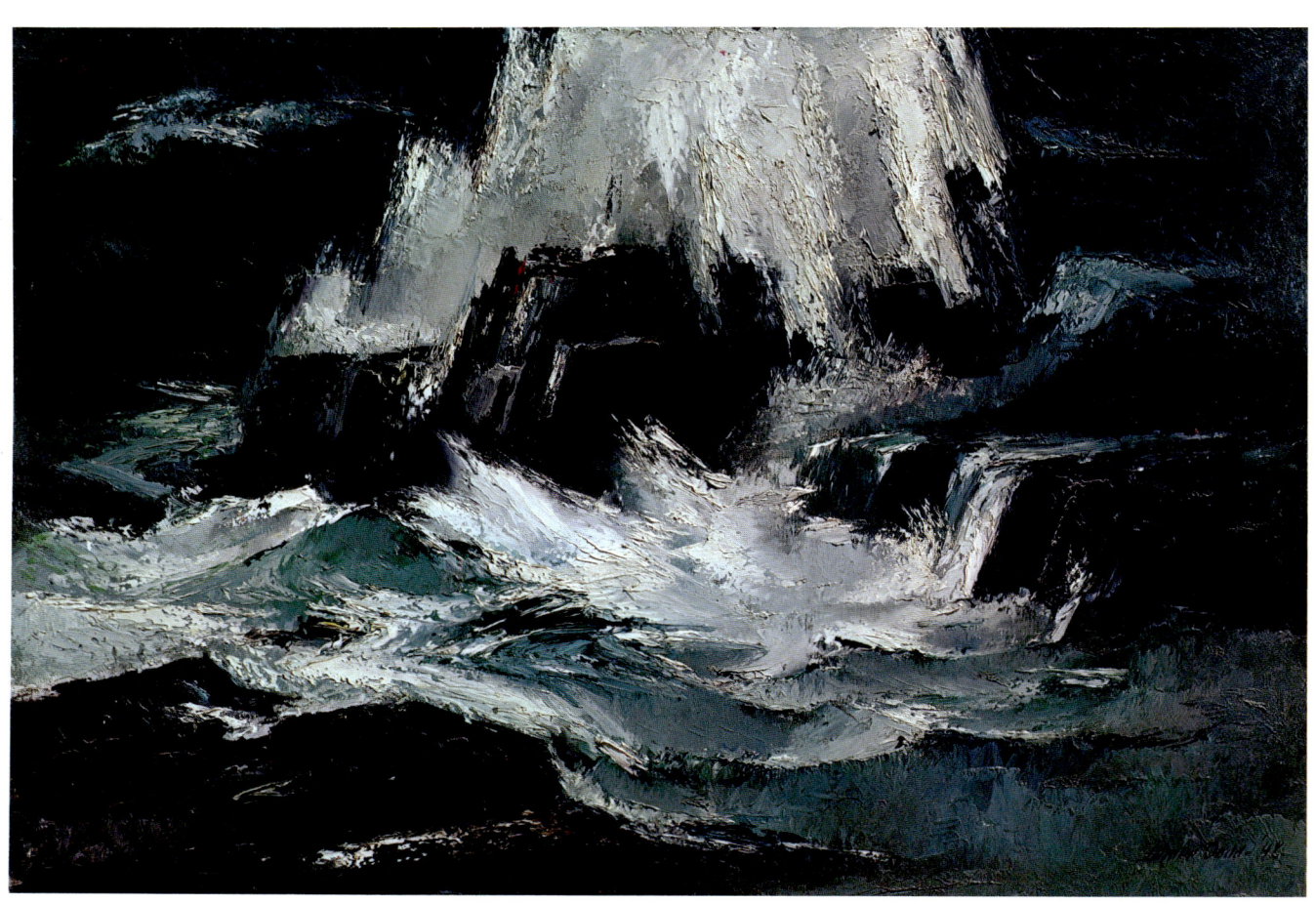

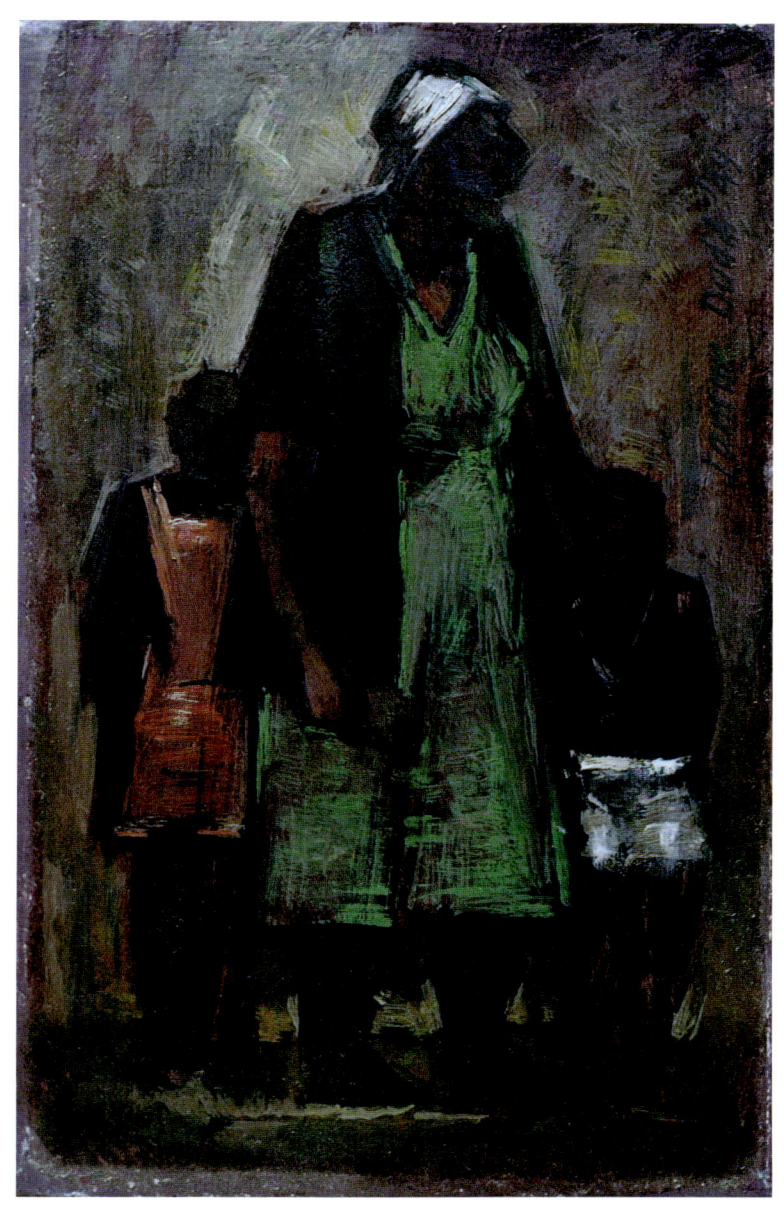

45. The White Door

Lent by The High Museum of Art, Atlanta

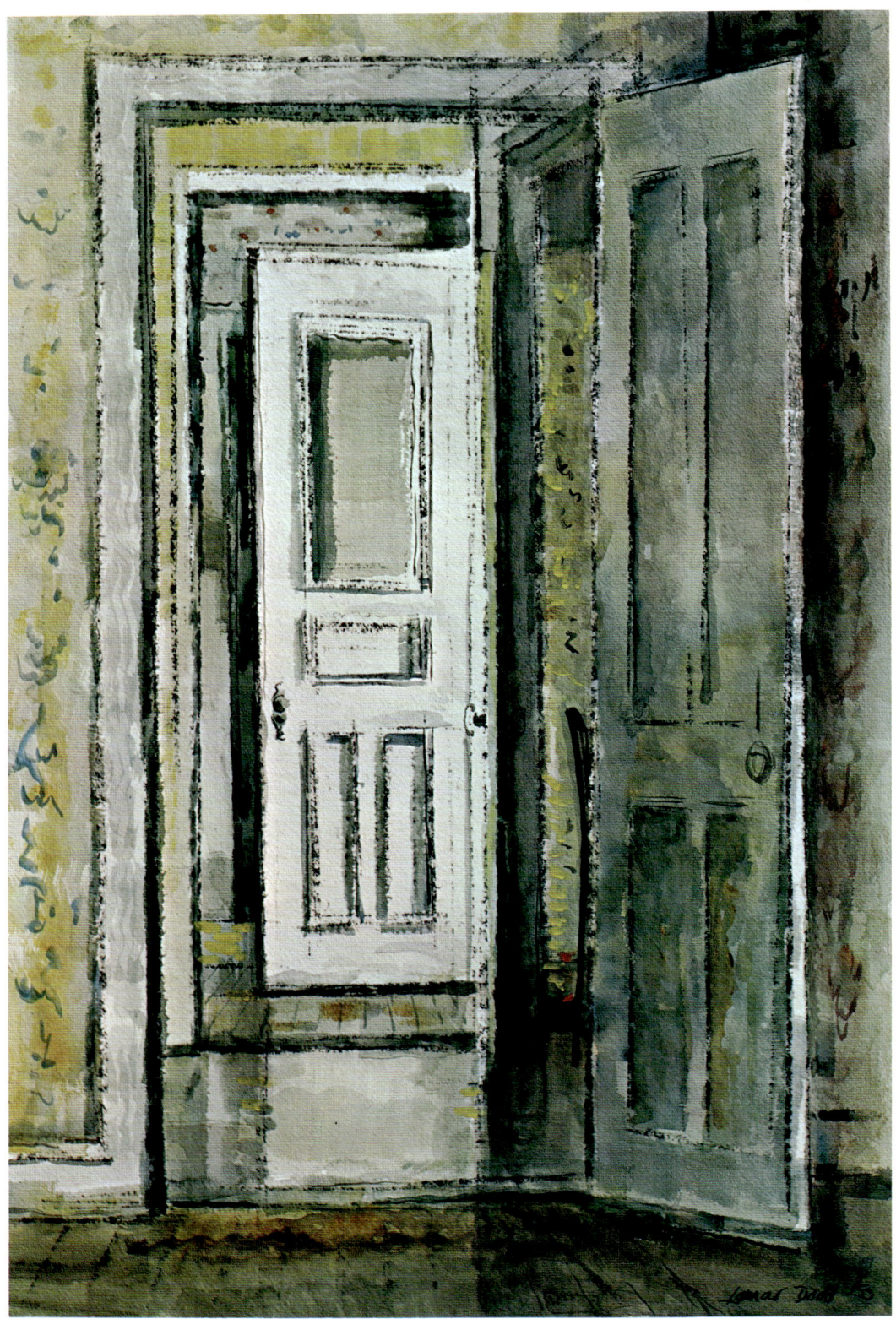

21. Still Life with Bottles

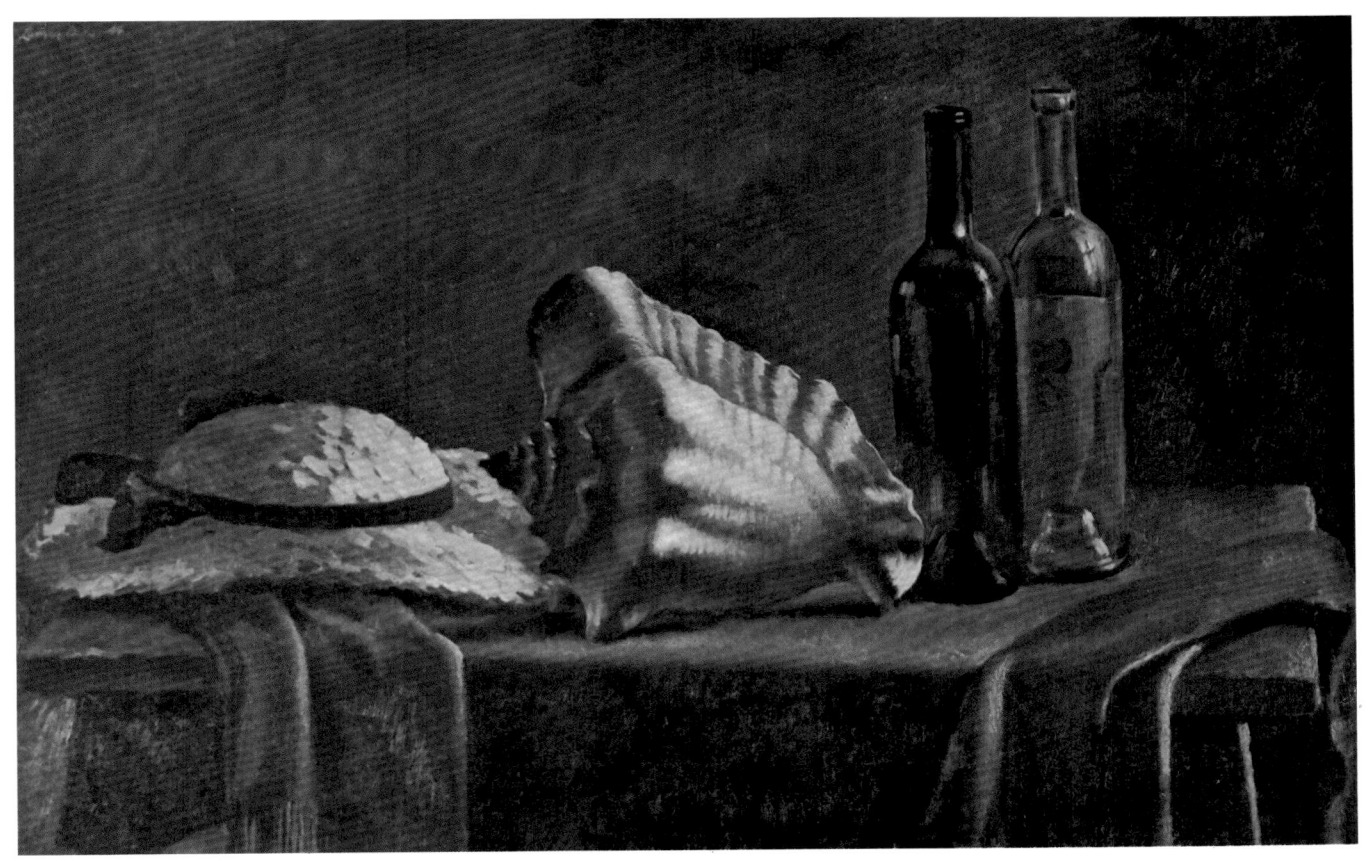

24. From this Earth

Lent by the Memorial Art Gallery of the University of Rochester, Rochester, New York. Marion Stratton Gould Fund

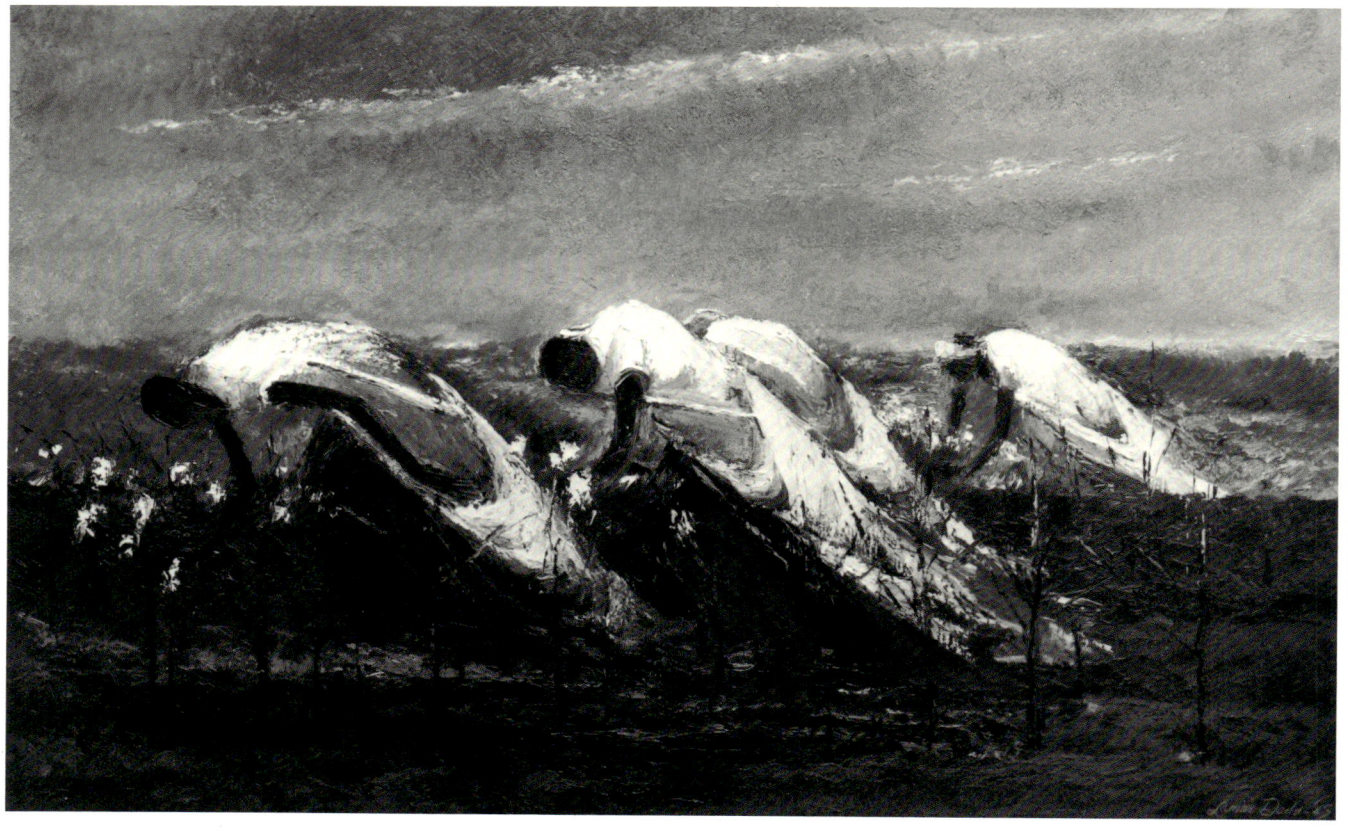

25. The Breaker

Lent by Galleries—Cranbrook Academy of Art, Bloomfield Hills, Michigan

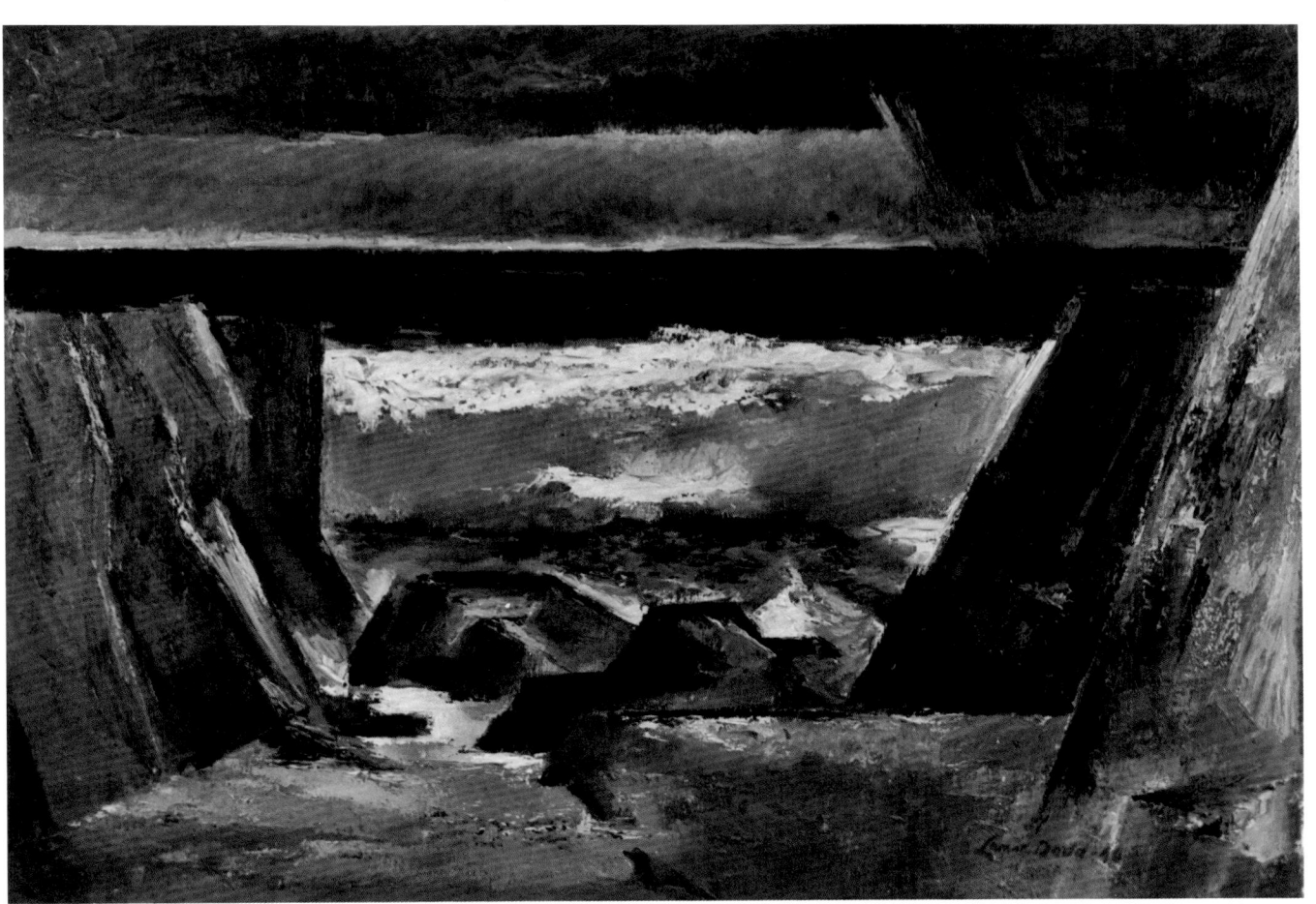

45   The Breaker

26. Lumpkin Street

Lent by Miss Barbara Stanwyck

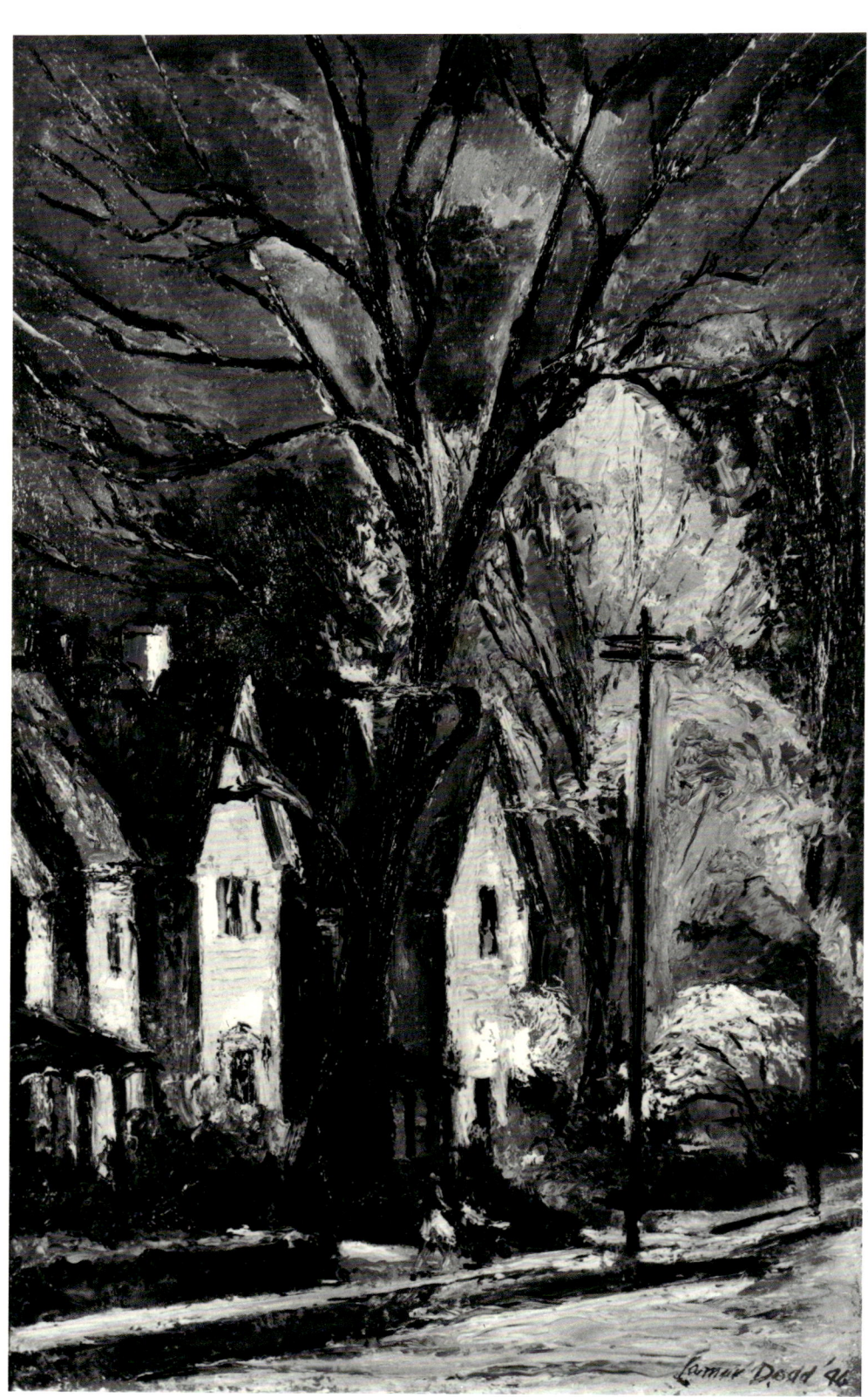

27. Savannah

Lent by The Montclair Art Museum, Montclair, New Jersey

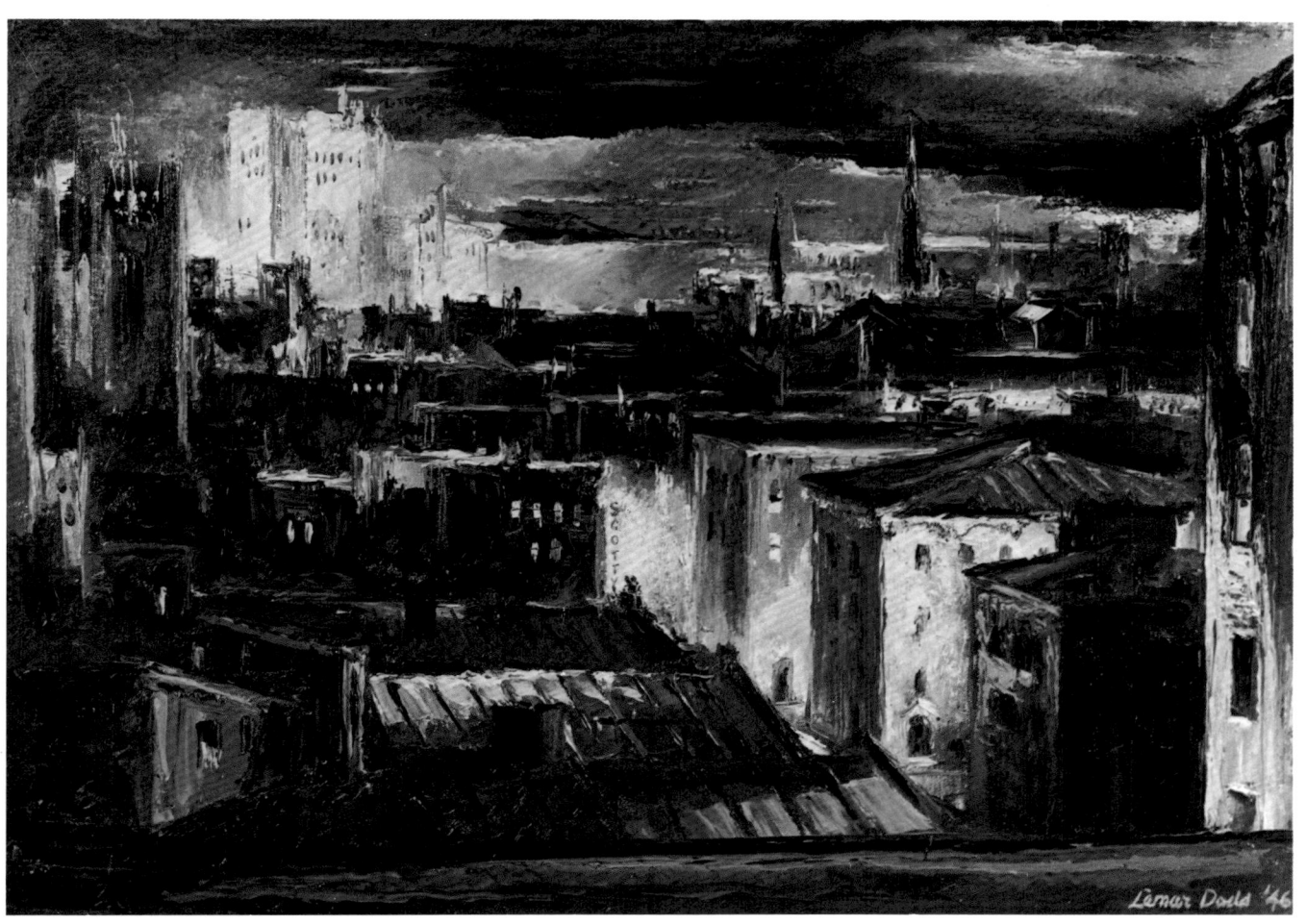

47.

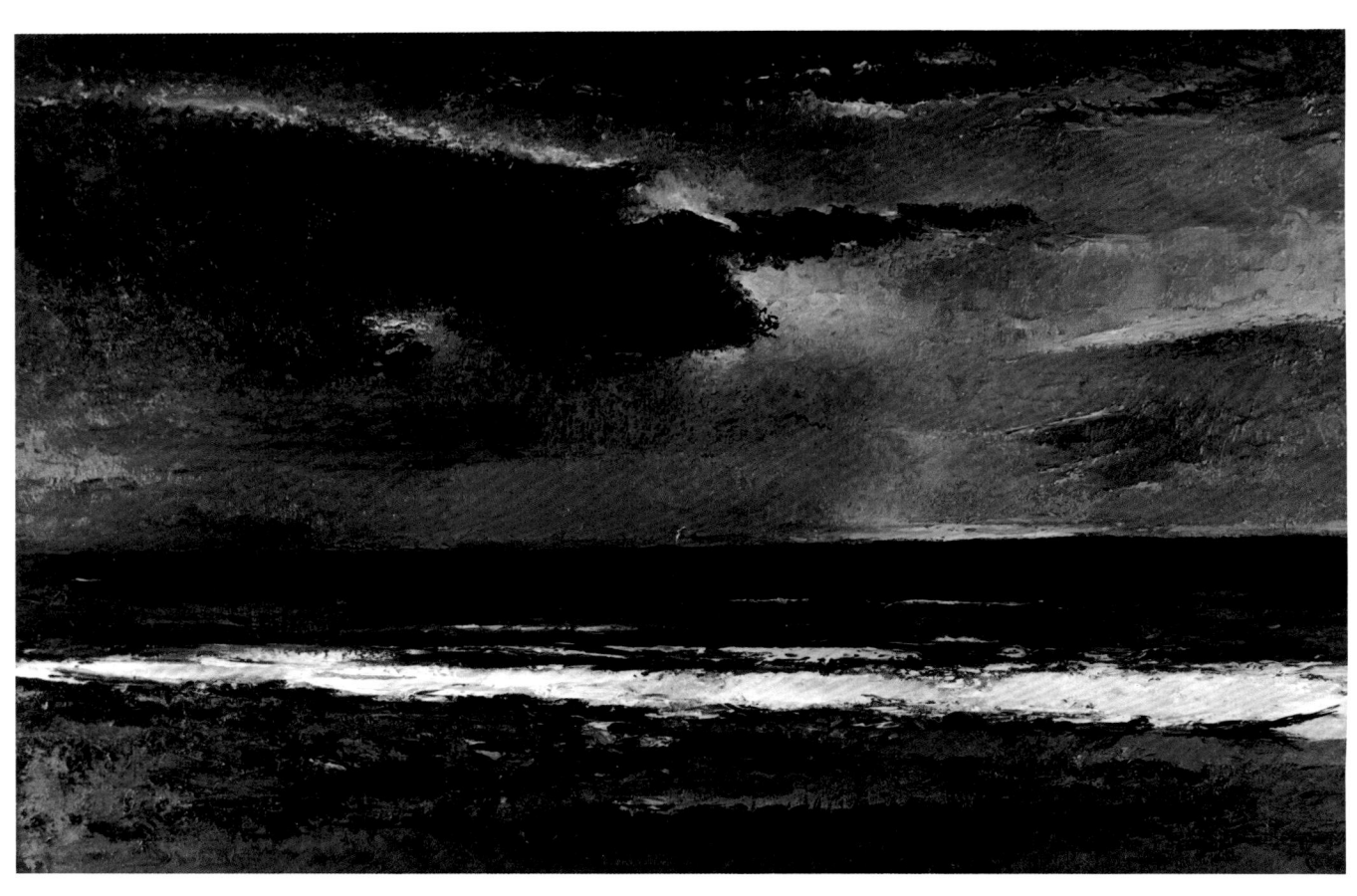

30. Objects on the Table

Lent by Mr. and Mrs. George W. Funderburk, Jr.

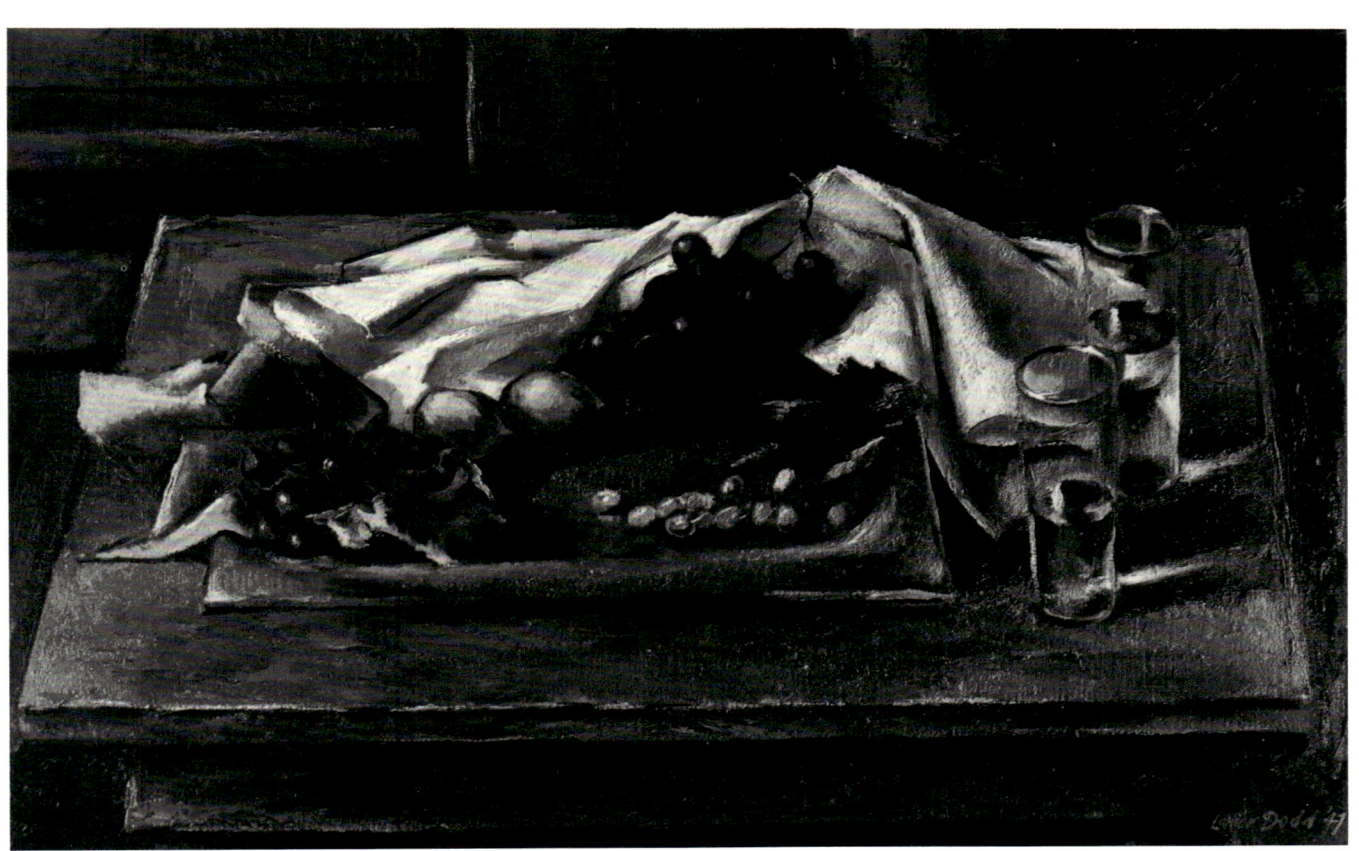

Objects on the Table

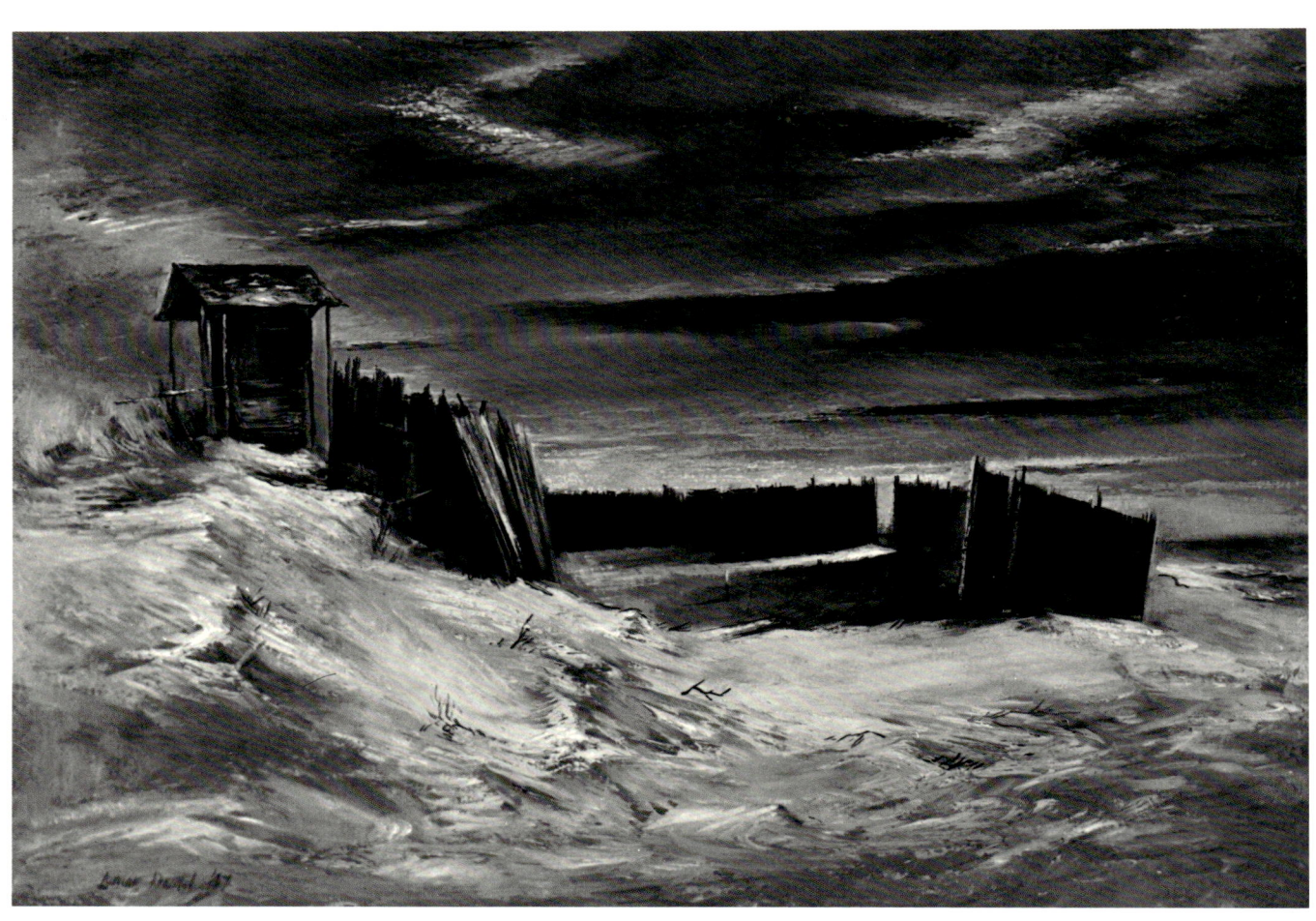

32. Winter Road

Lent by the Virginia Museum of Fine Arts, Richmond, Virginia

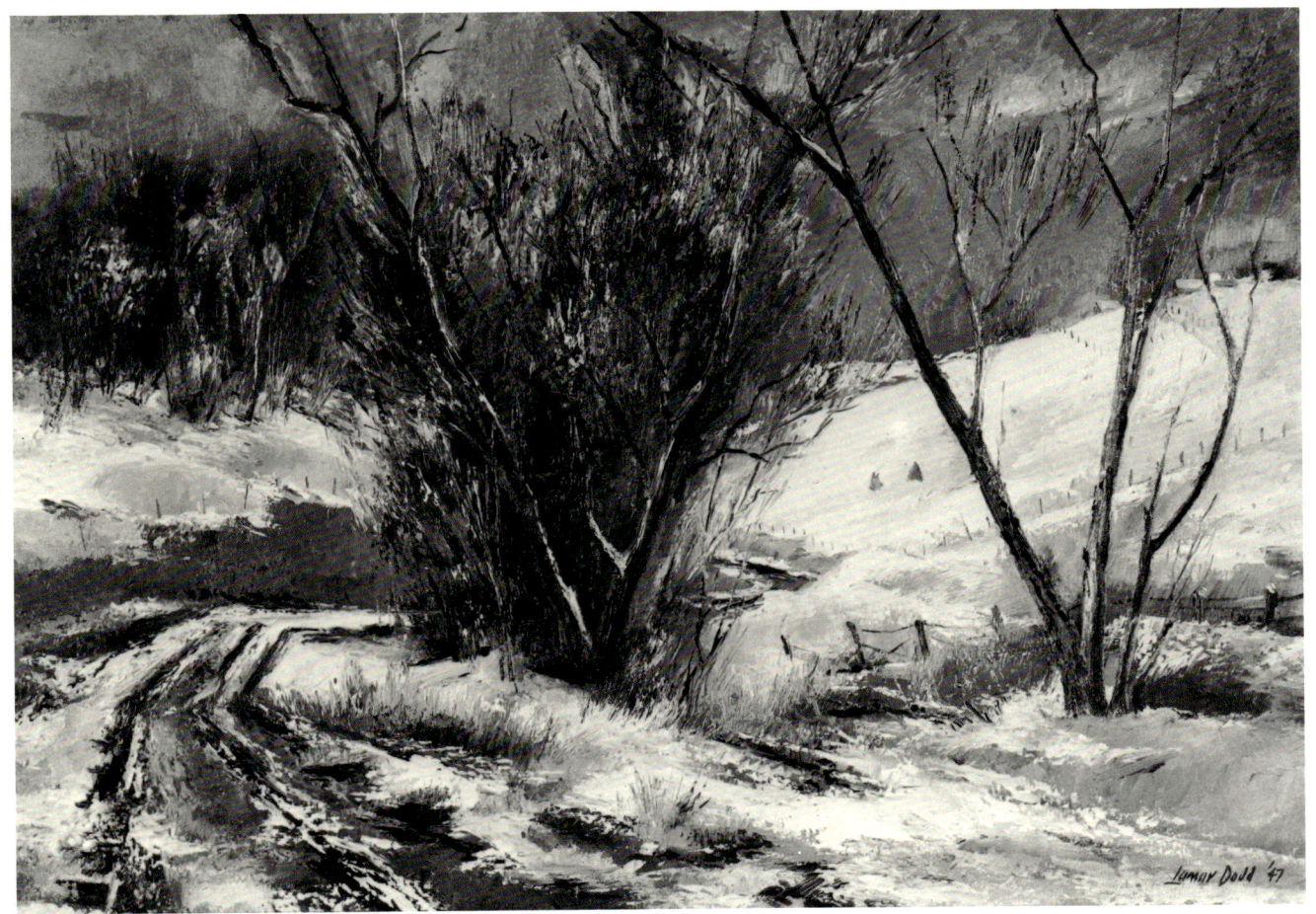

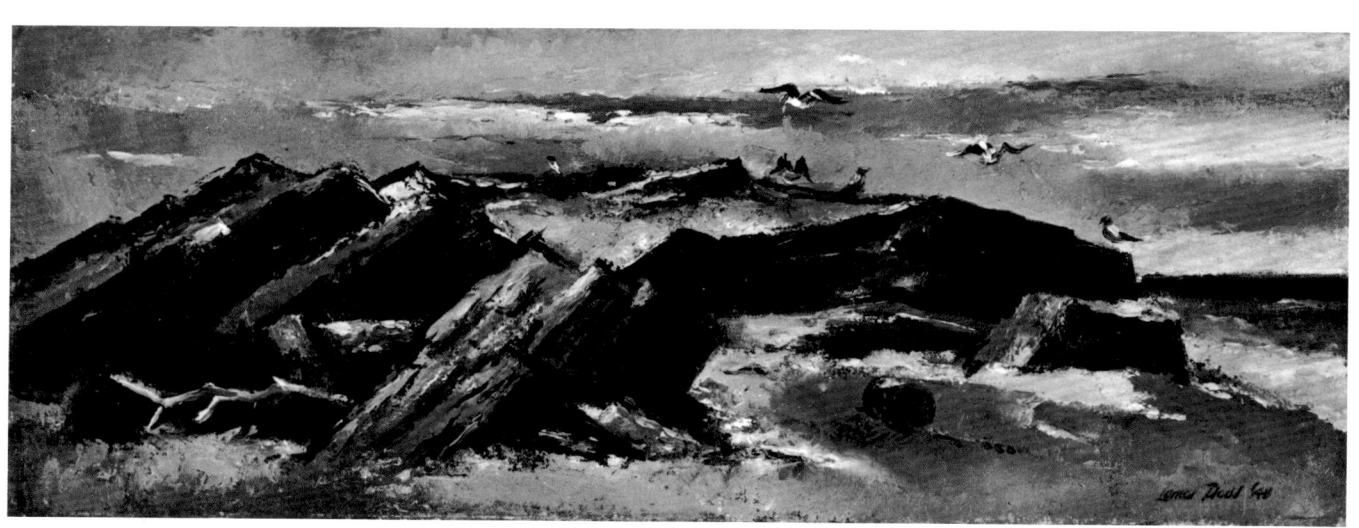

Along the Harbor

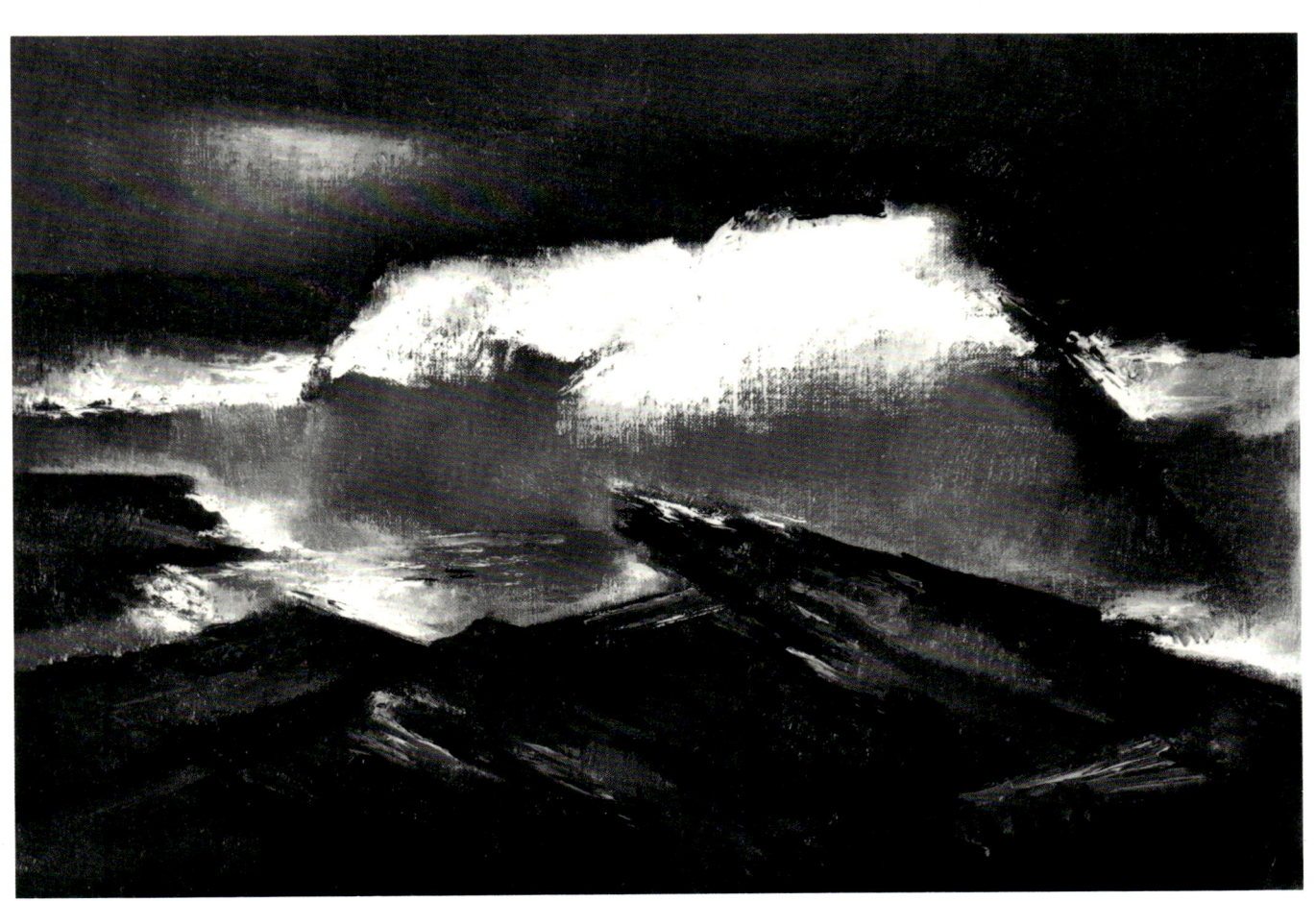

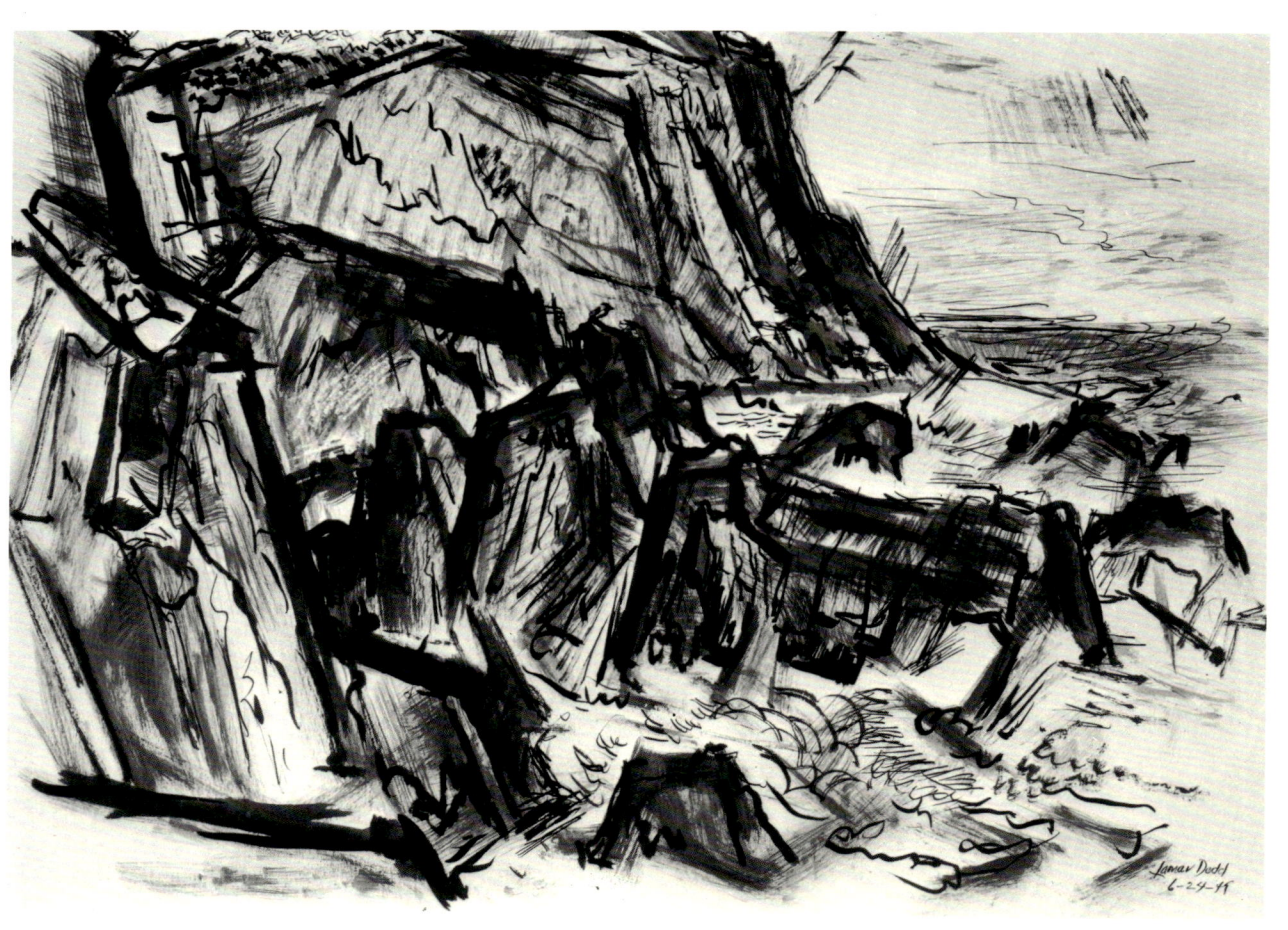

38. Monhegan Theme

Lent by The Metropolitan Museum of Art,
George A. Hearn Fund, 1951.

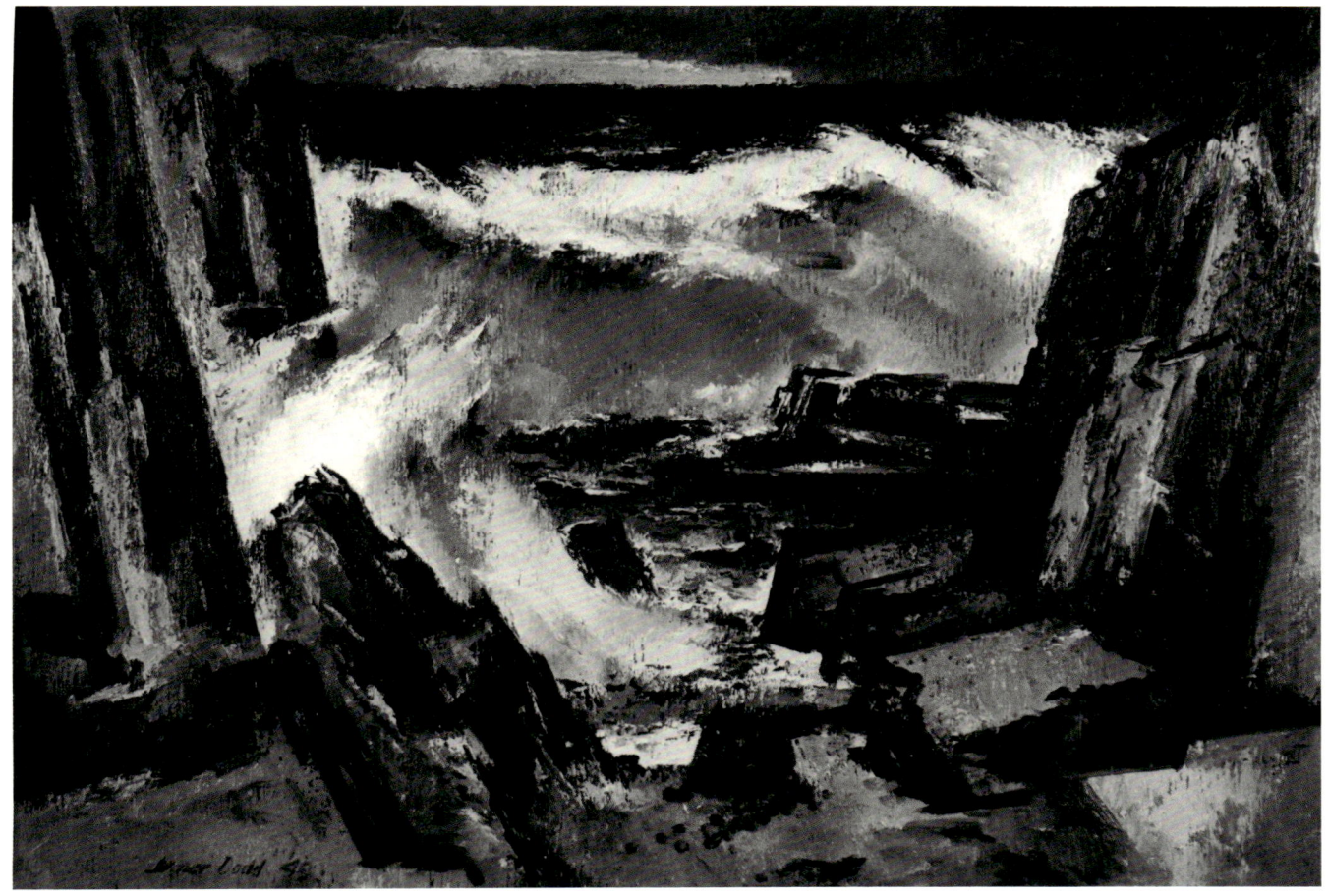

55.

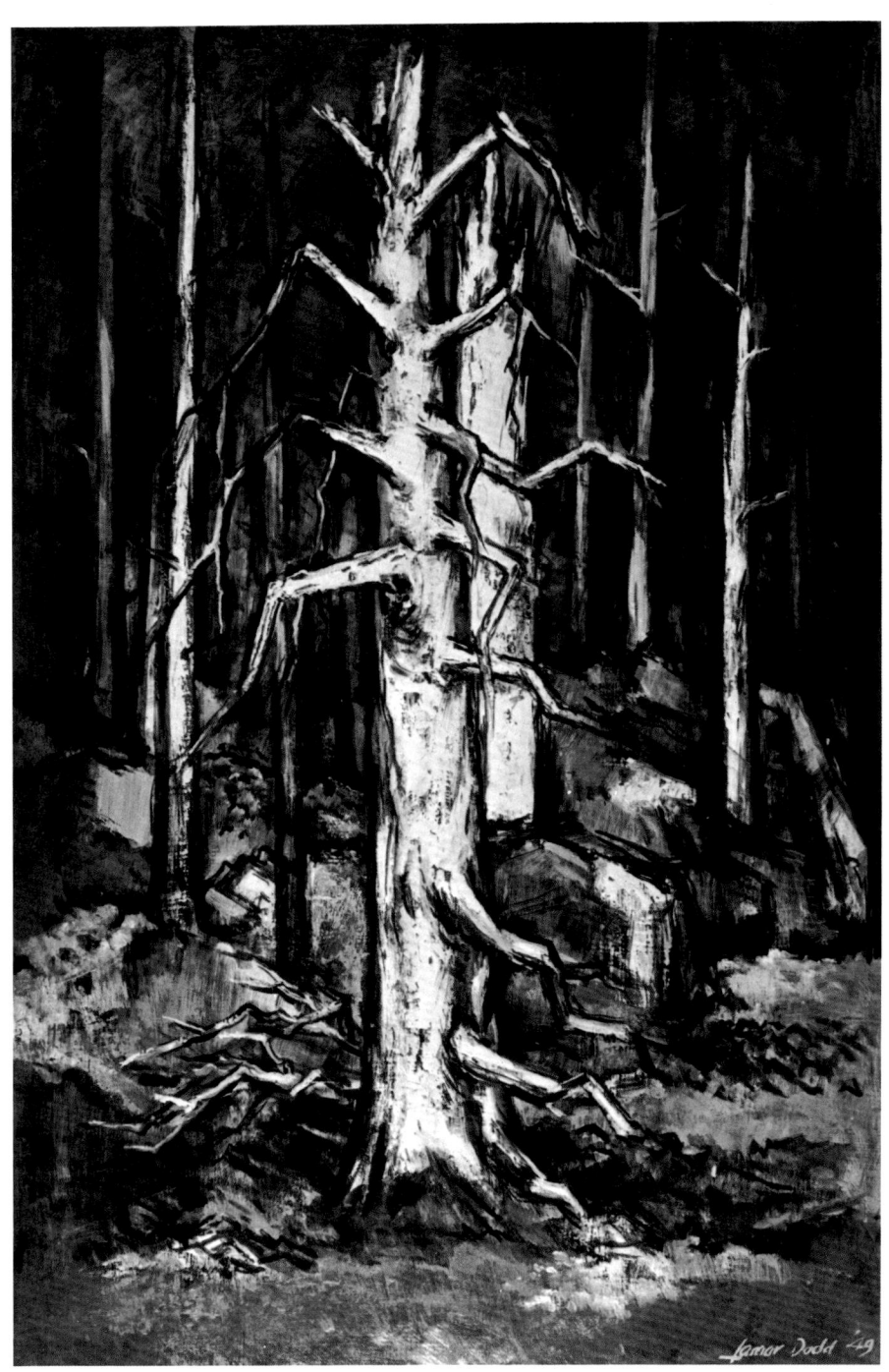

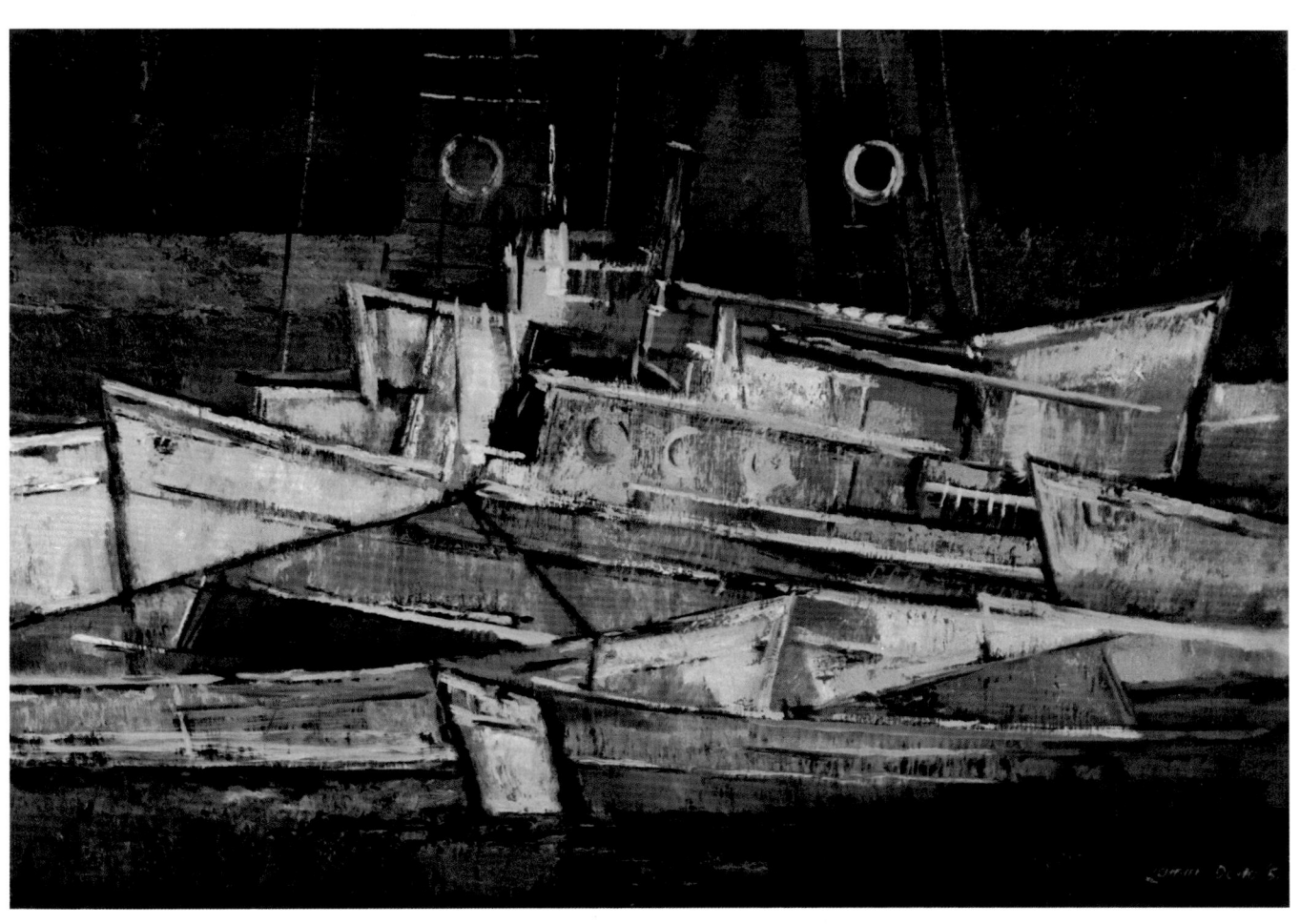

Of the Sea

41. Aspiring

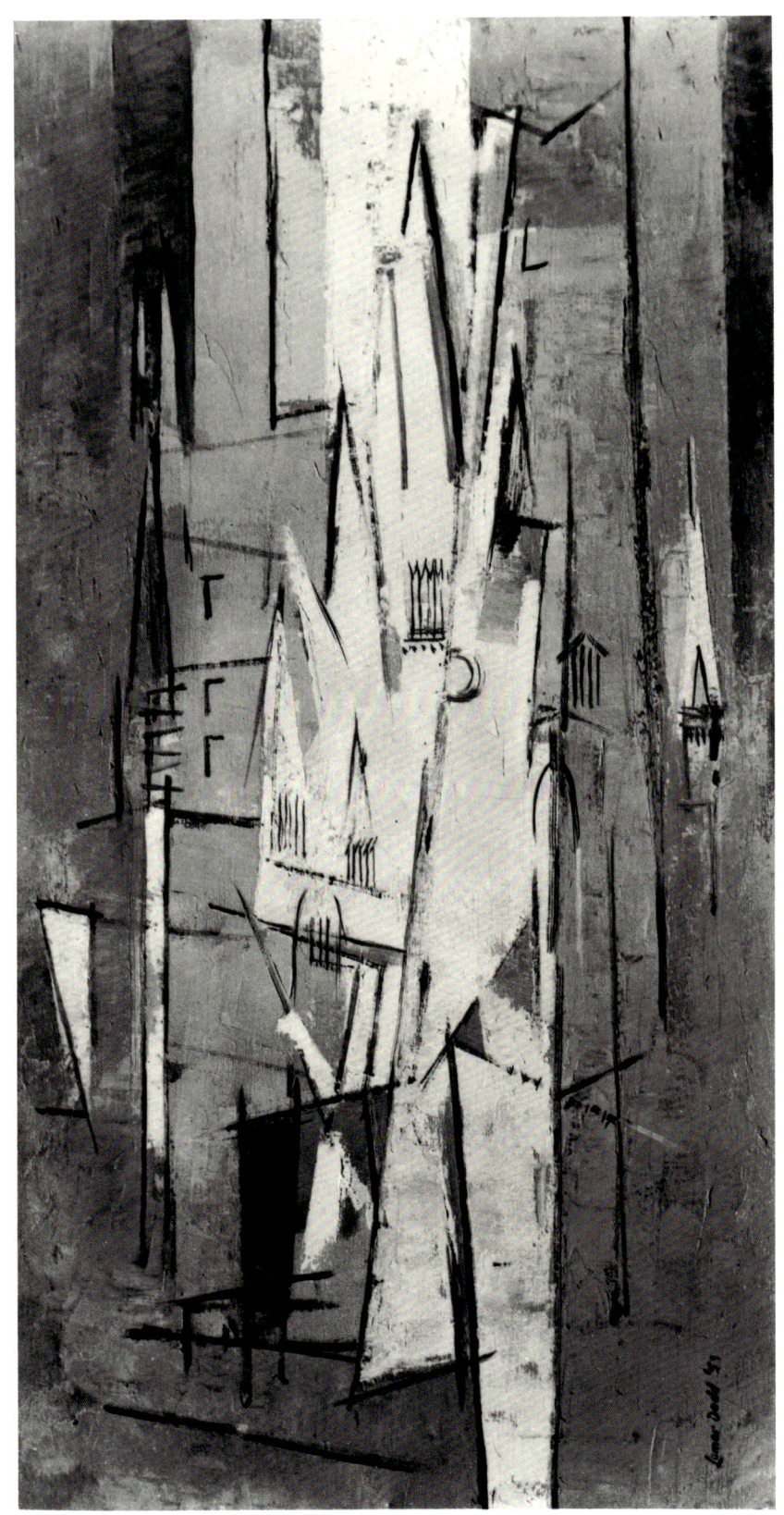

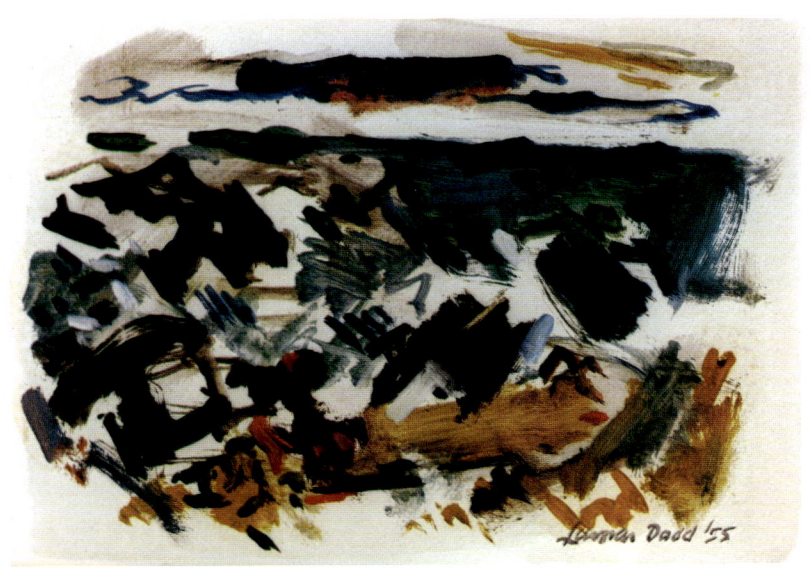

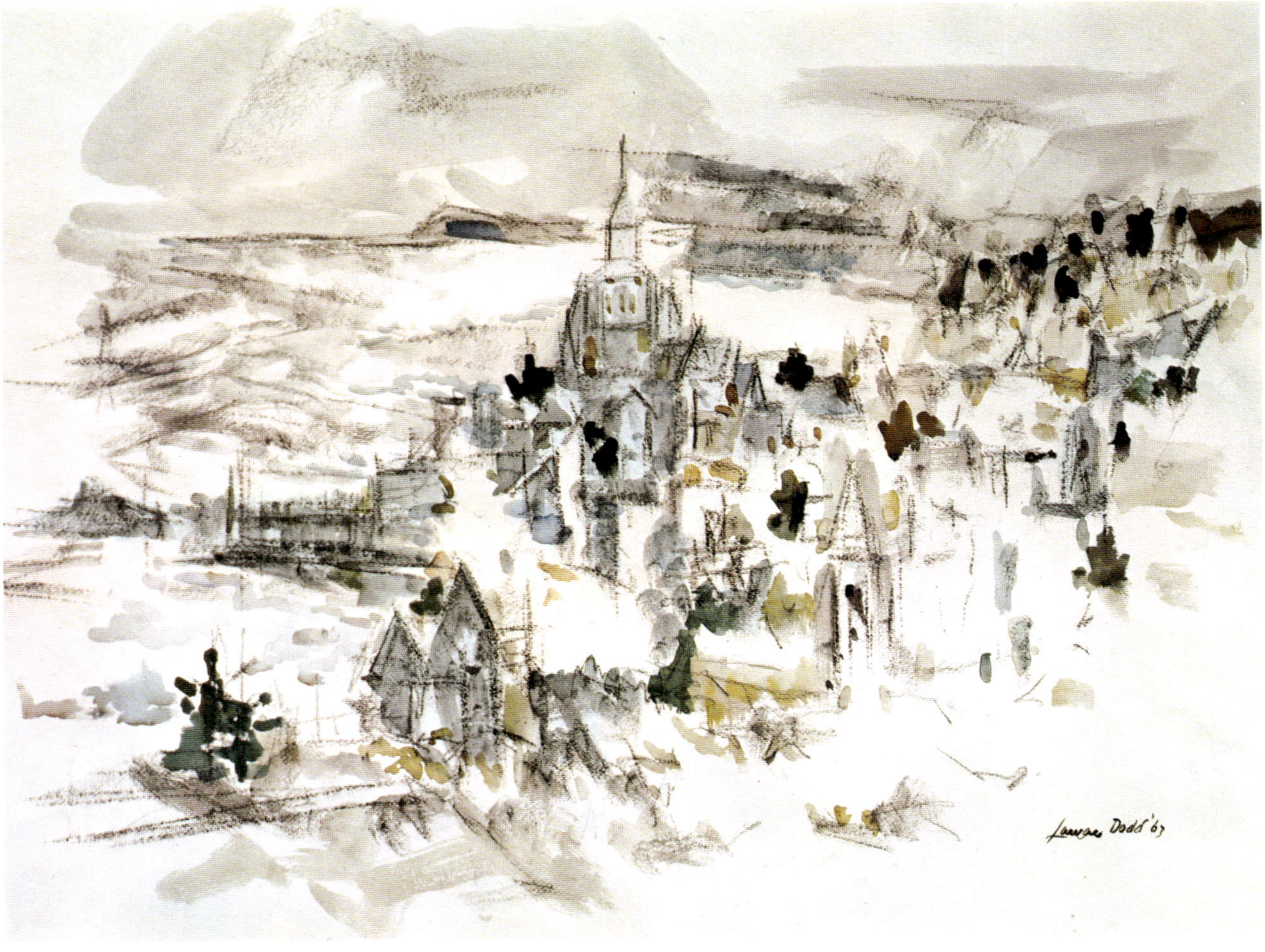

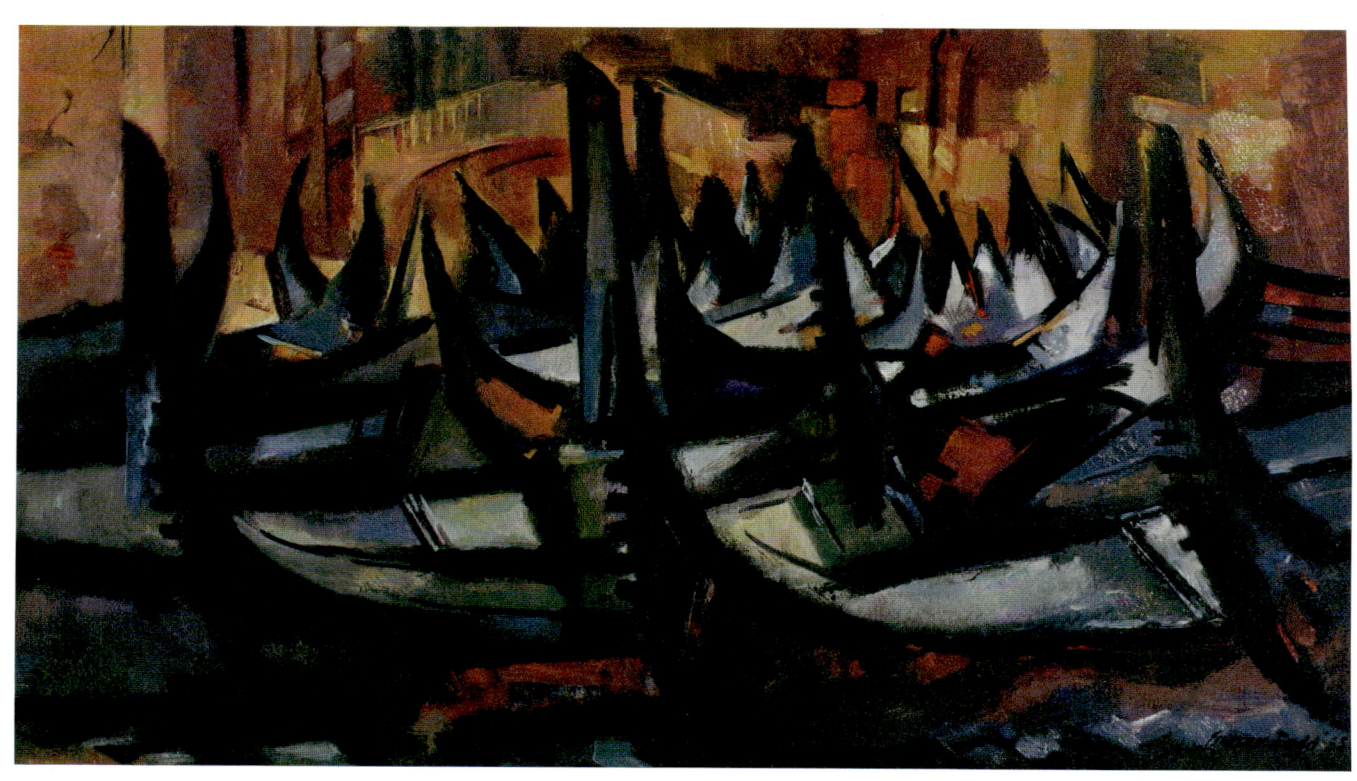

Lent by Lehigh University Permanent Collection. 1958. Ralph Wilson Fund

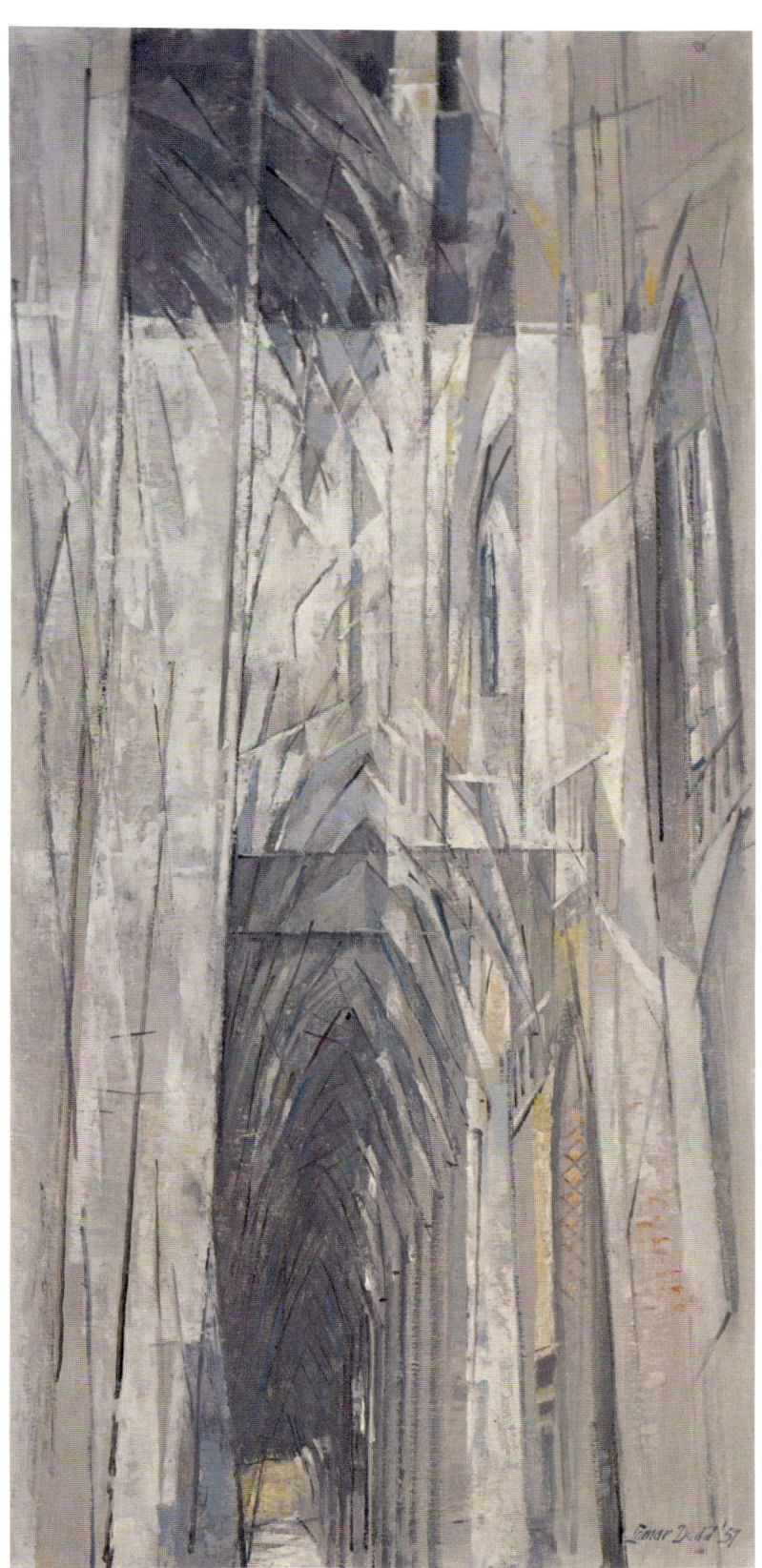

Cathedral #1

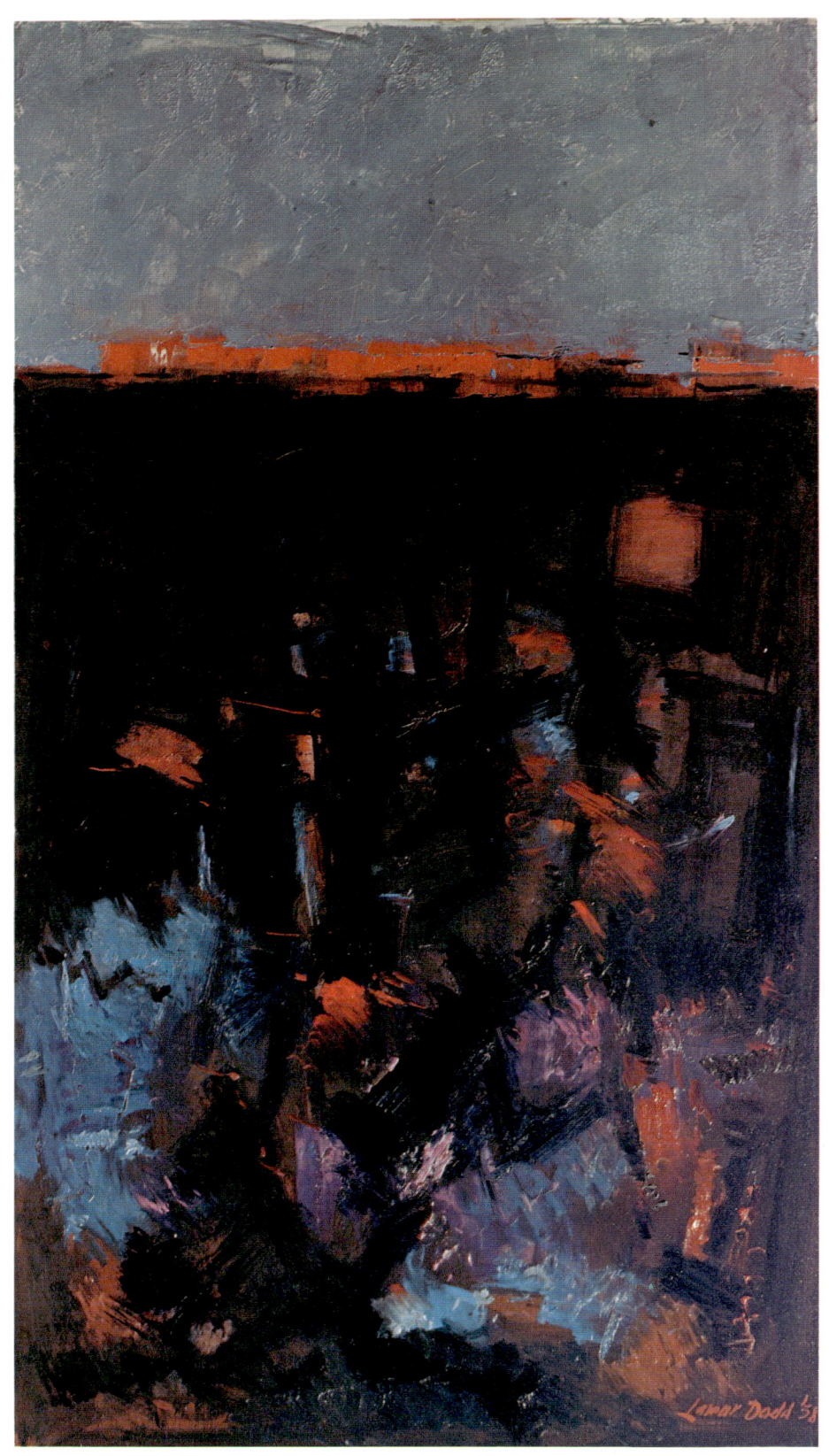

42. The Elements

Lent by Dr. and Mrs. Morris B. Abram

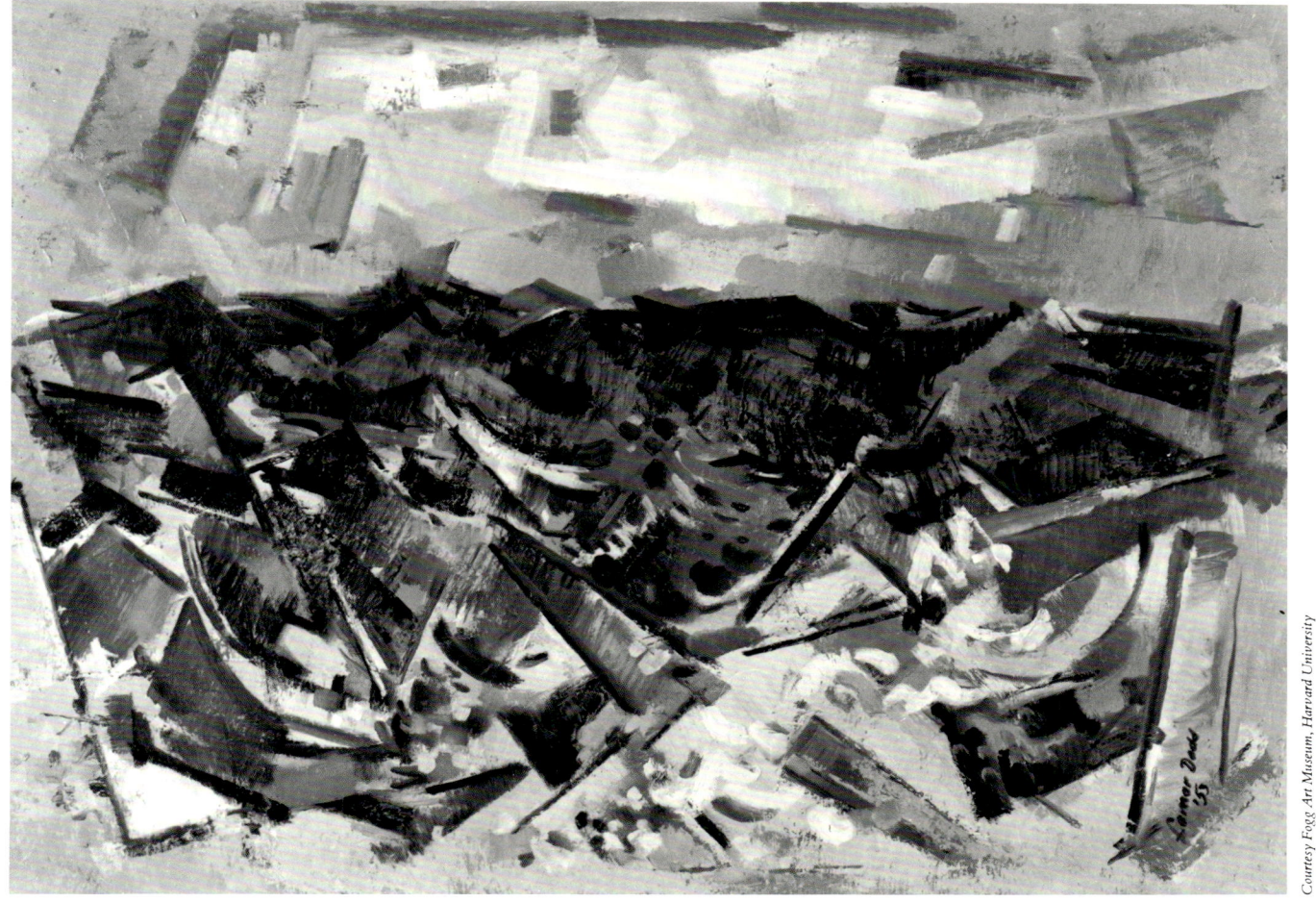

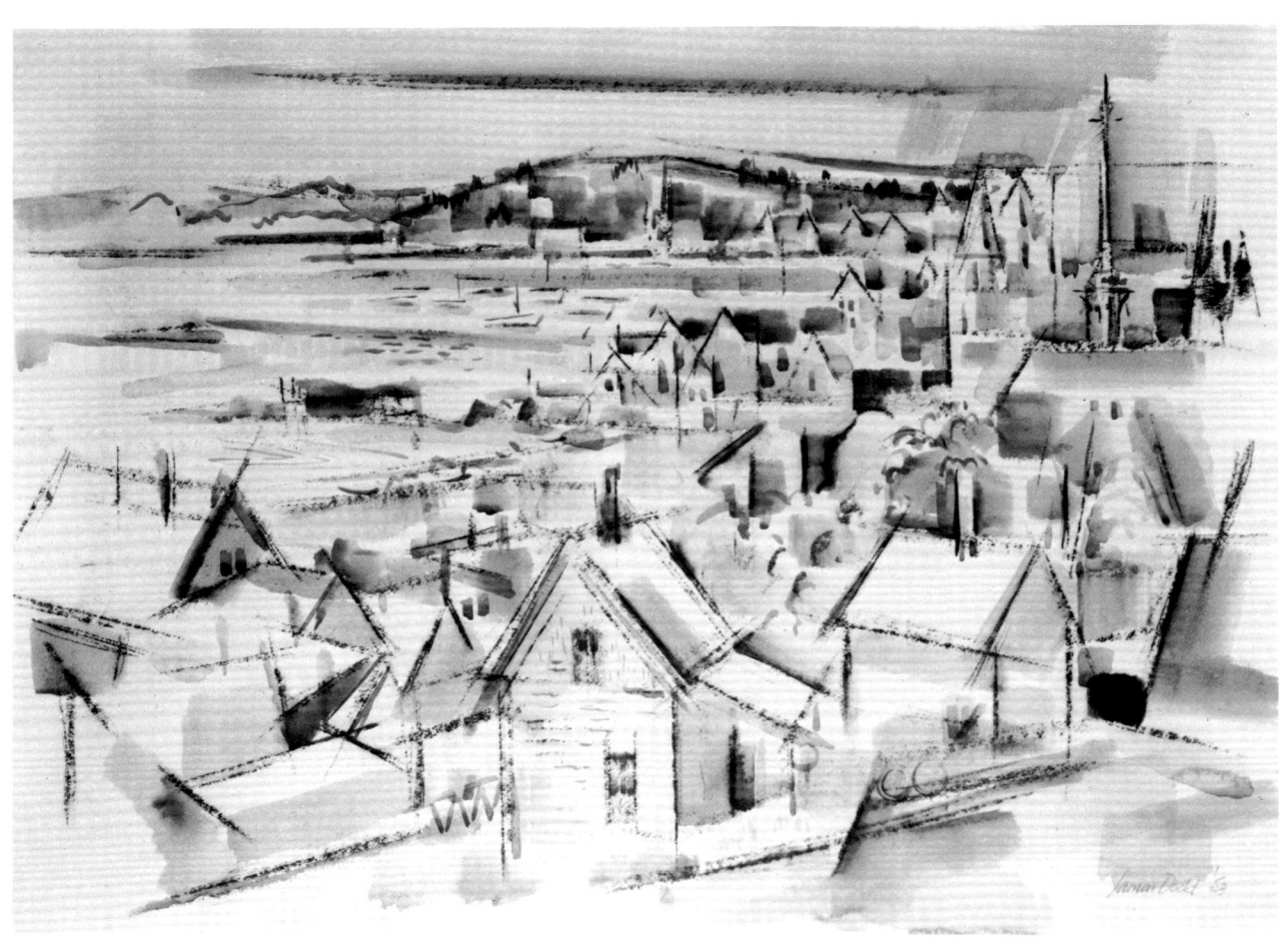

46. Wolf Fork Valley

Lent by Mr. and Mrs. W. Porter Kellam

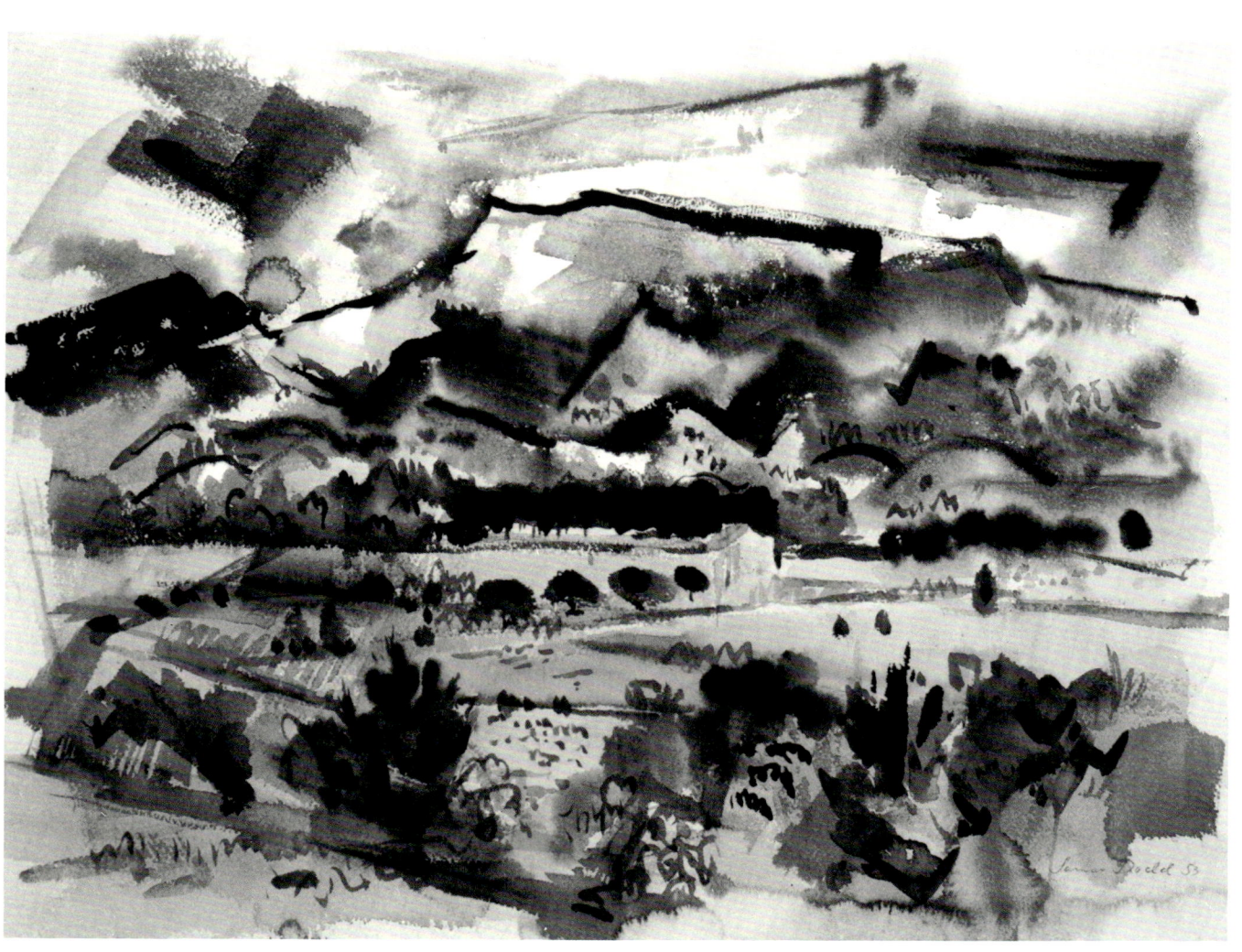

47. Italian Village #2

Collection of The Nebraska Art Association, courtesy Sheldon Memorial Art Gallery, The University of Nebraska, Lincoln, Nebraska

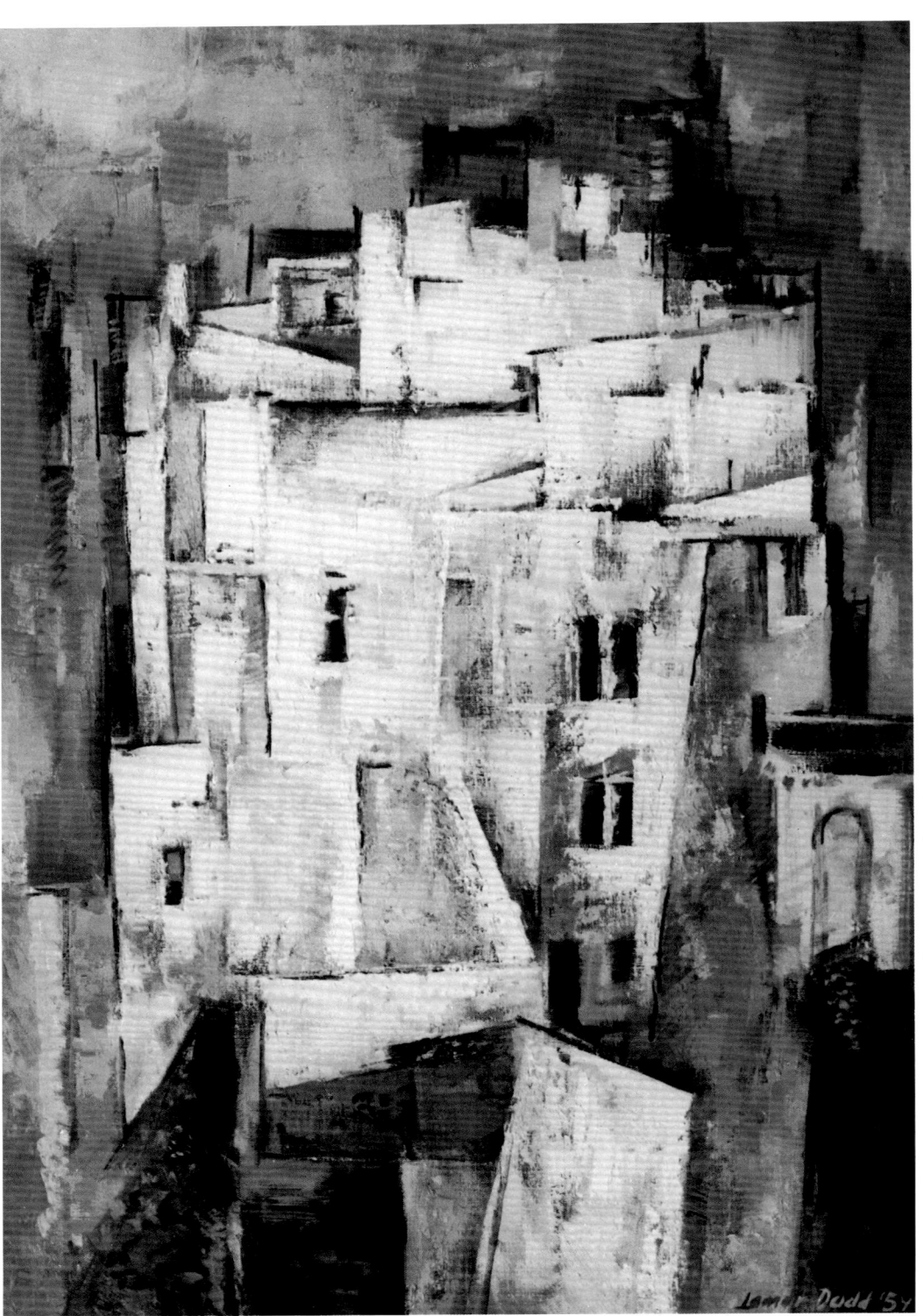

52. Venetian Patterns

Lent by Columbus Museum of Arts and Crafts, Columbus, Georgia

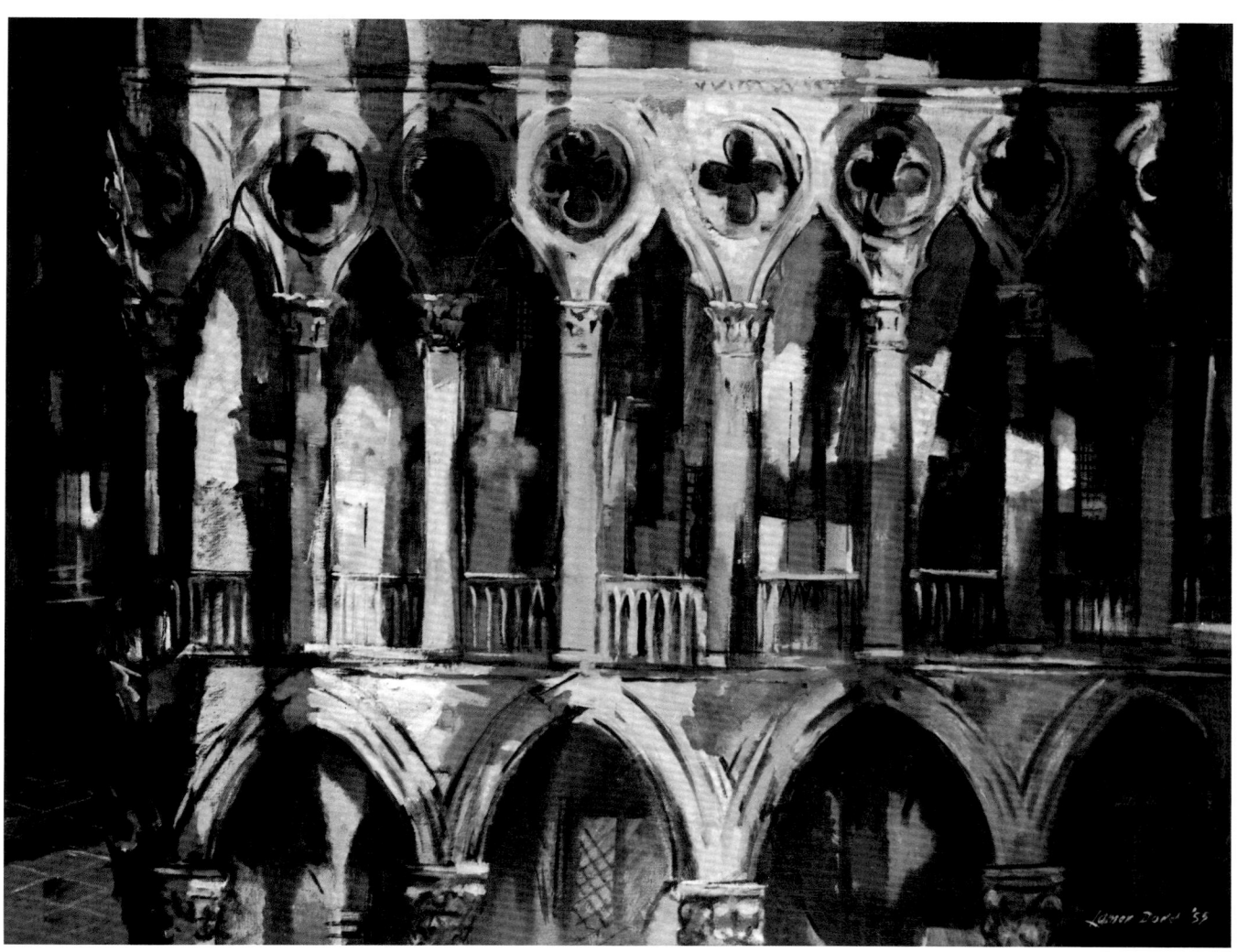

Venetian Patterns

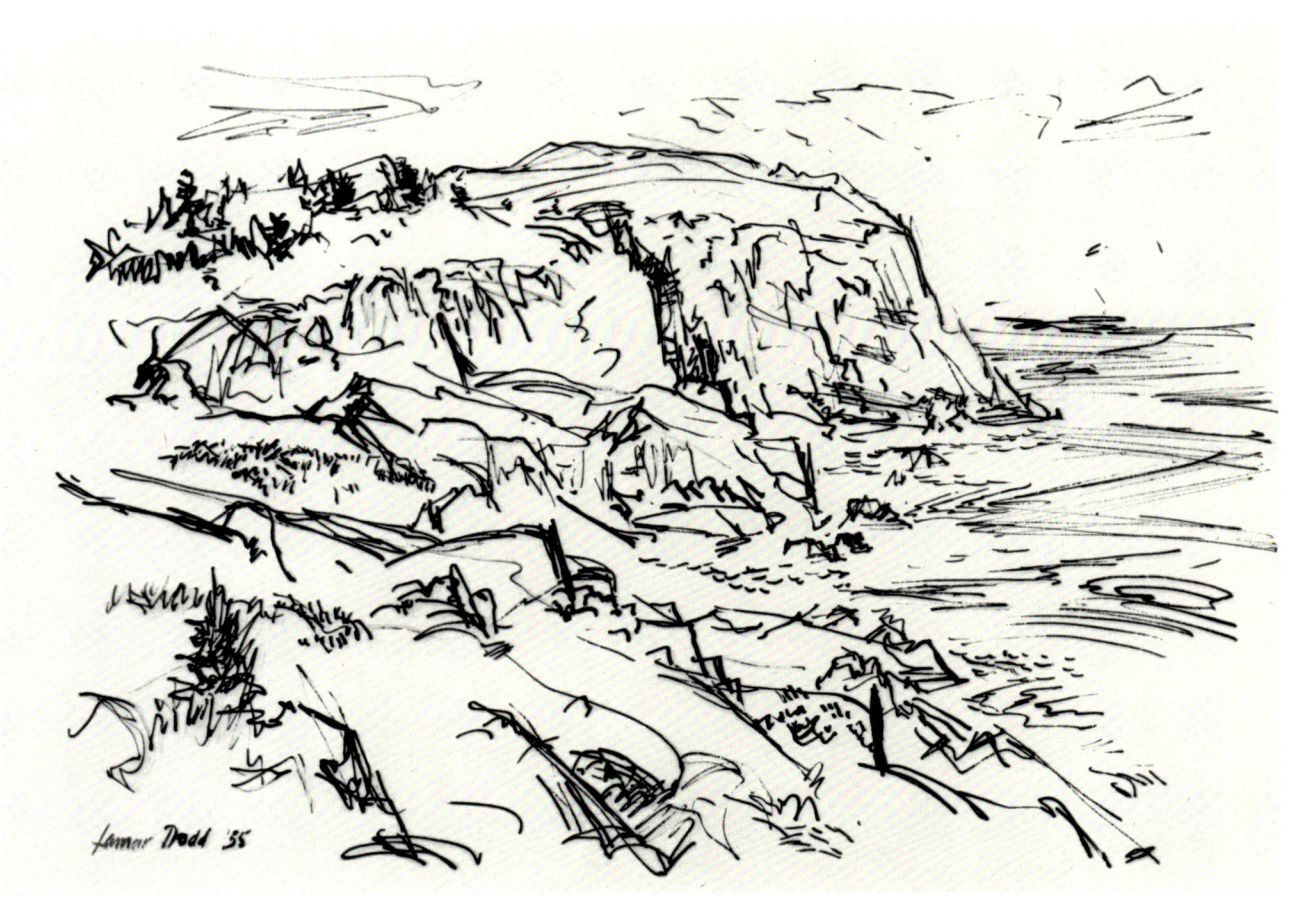

54. Cathedral Soliloquy

Lent by Grand Rapids Art Museum, Grand Rapids, Michigan

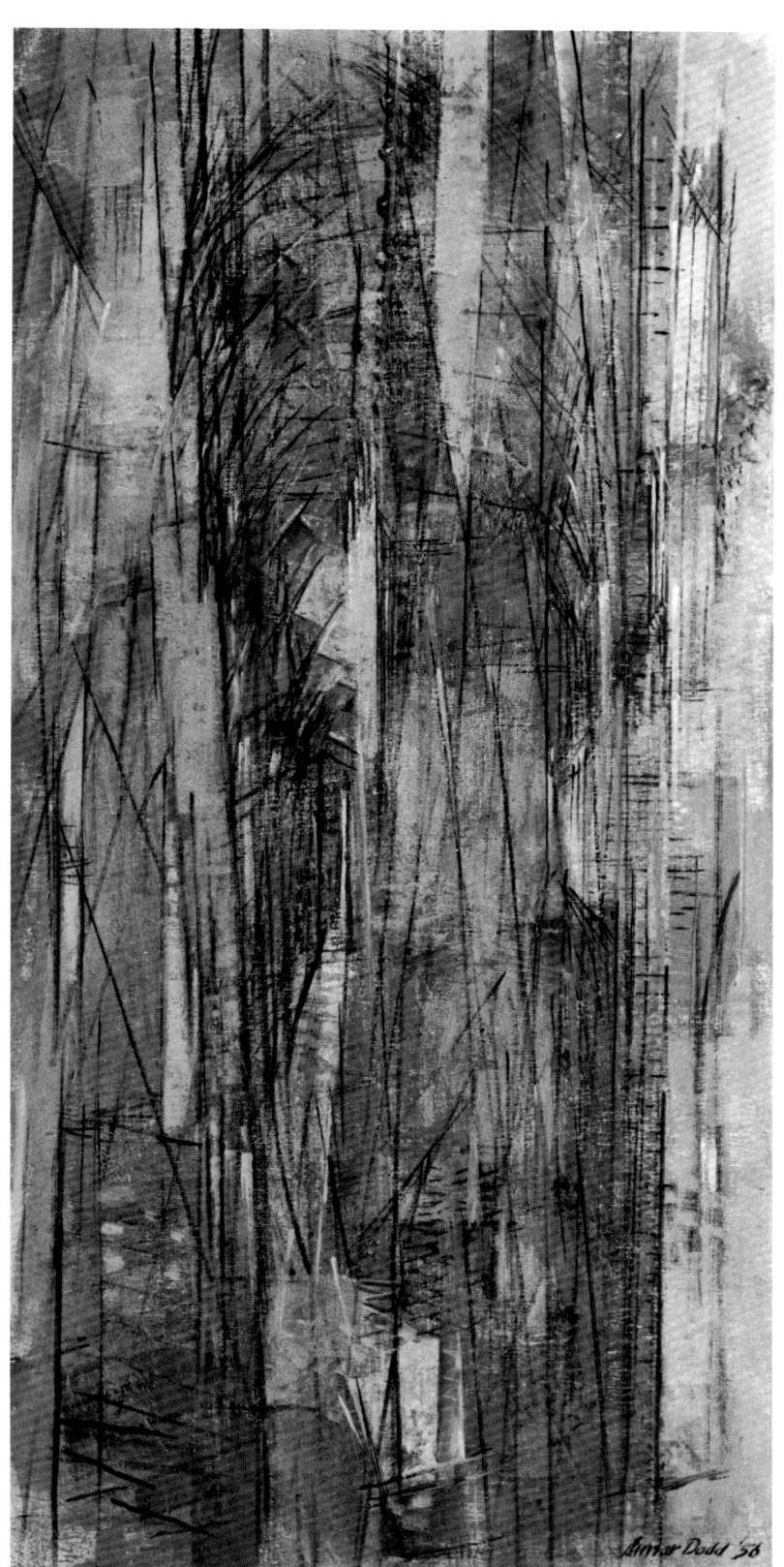

Cathedral Soliloquy

55. Piazza San Marco

Lent by Mrs. John S. Dodd, Sr.

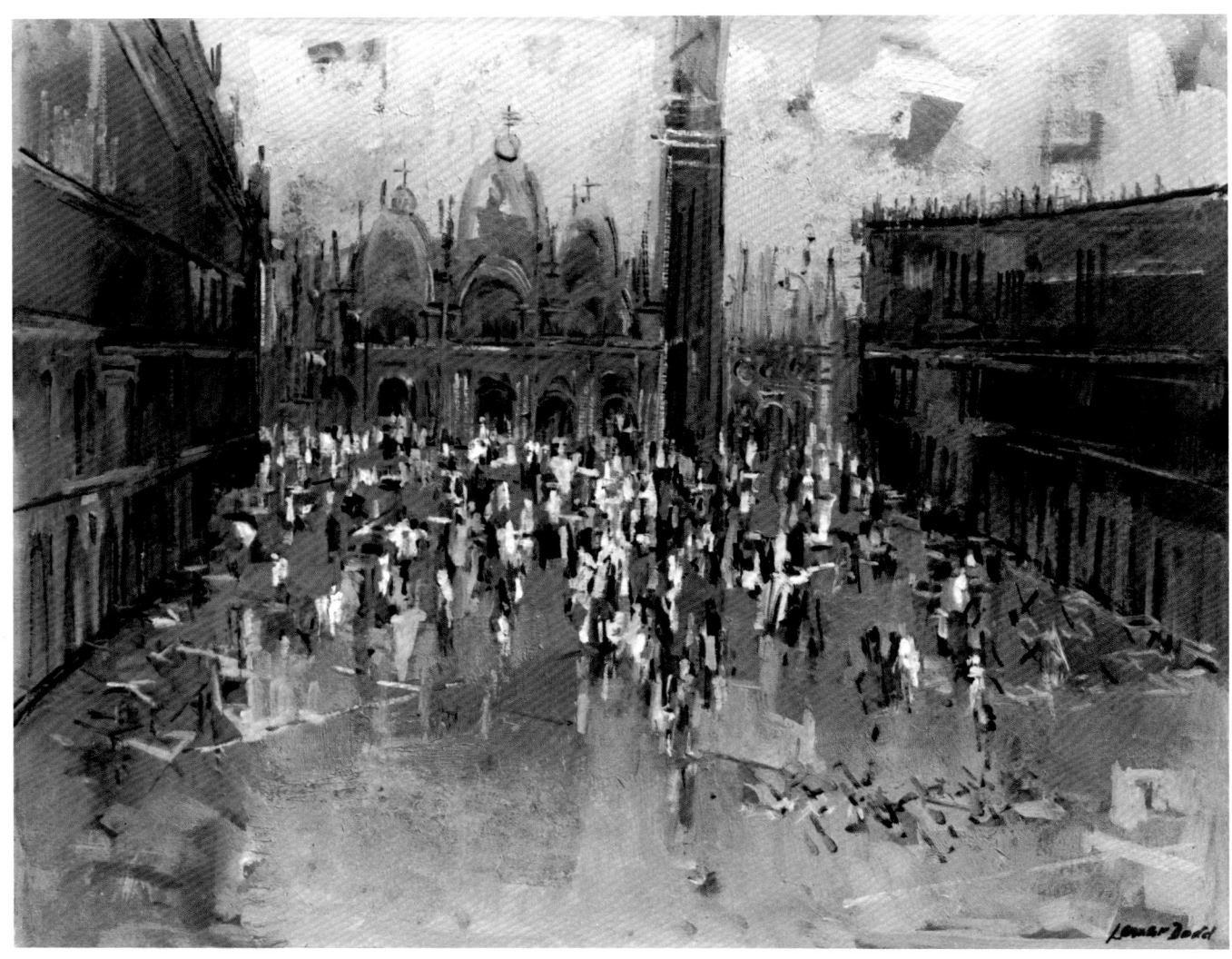

56. St. Mark's Cathedral

Lent by Mr. and Mrs. William J. Cabin

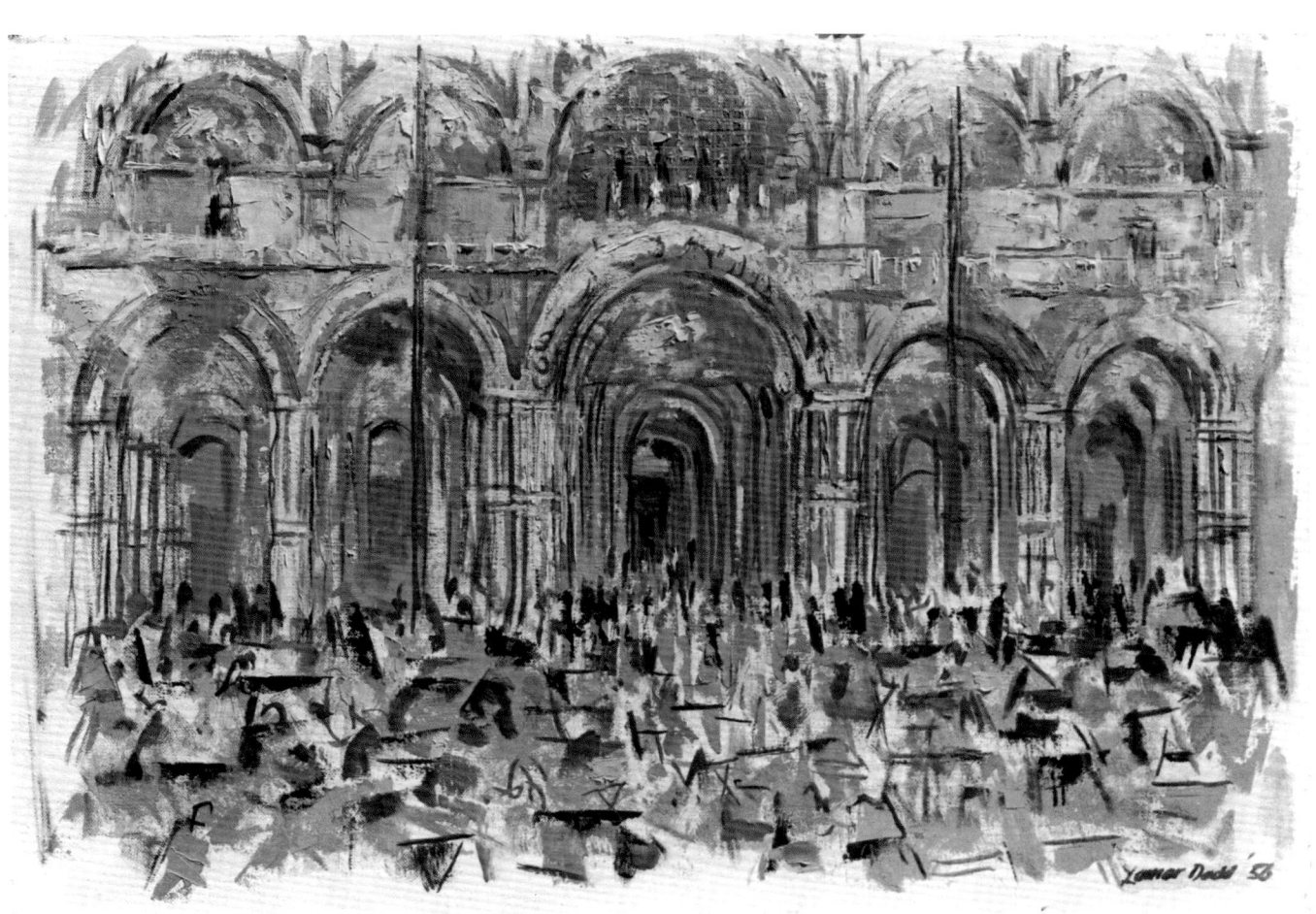

57. They Come, They Go

Lent by Grand Central Art Galleries, New York

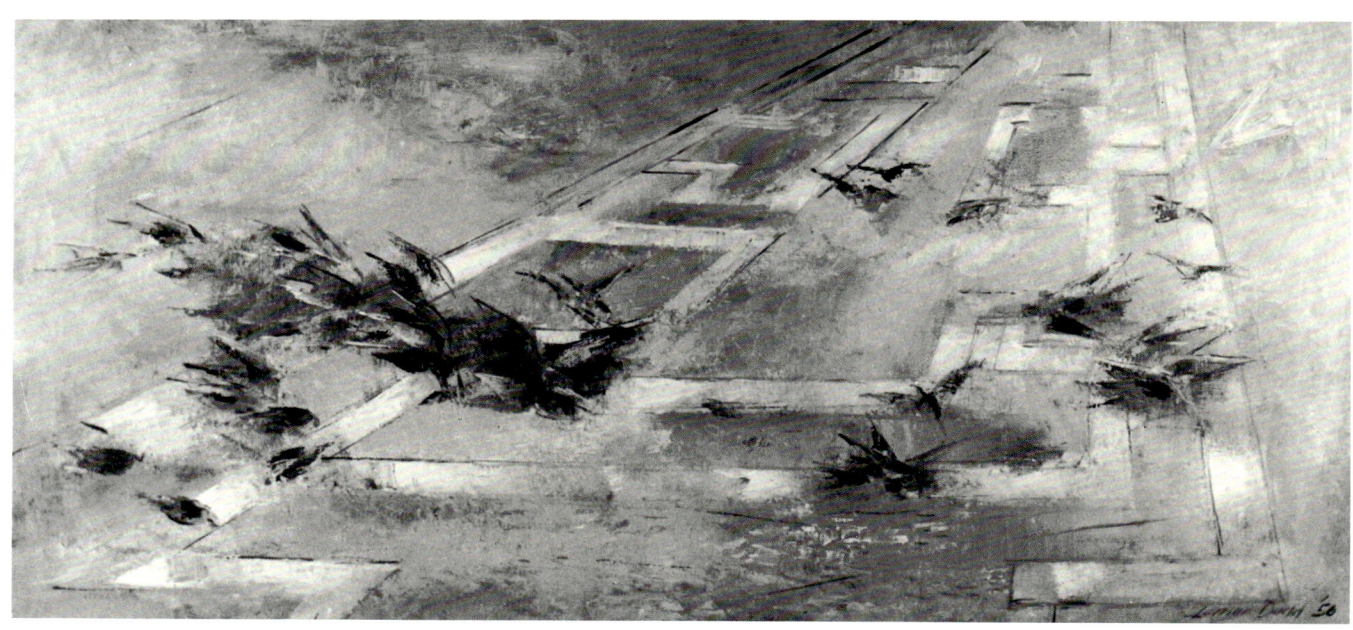

They Come, They Go

58. Across the Bosphorus

Lent by Pennsylvania Academy of the Fine Arts, Philadelphia, Pennsylvania

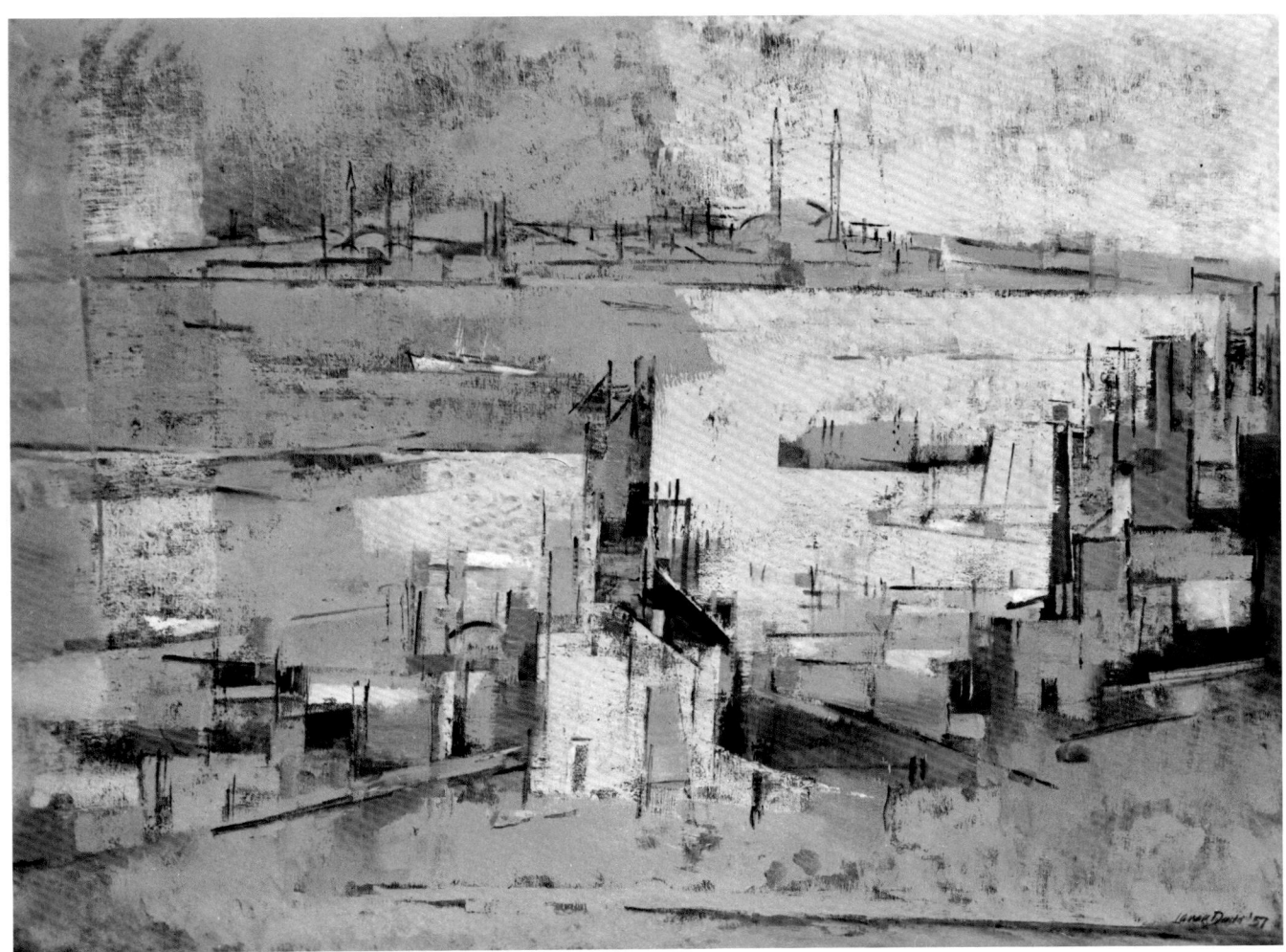

Across the Bosphorus

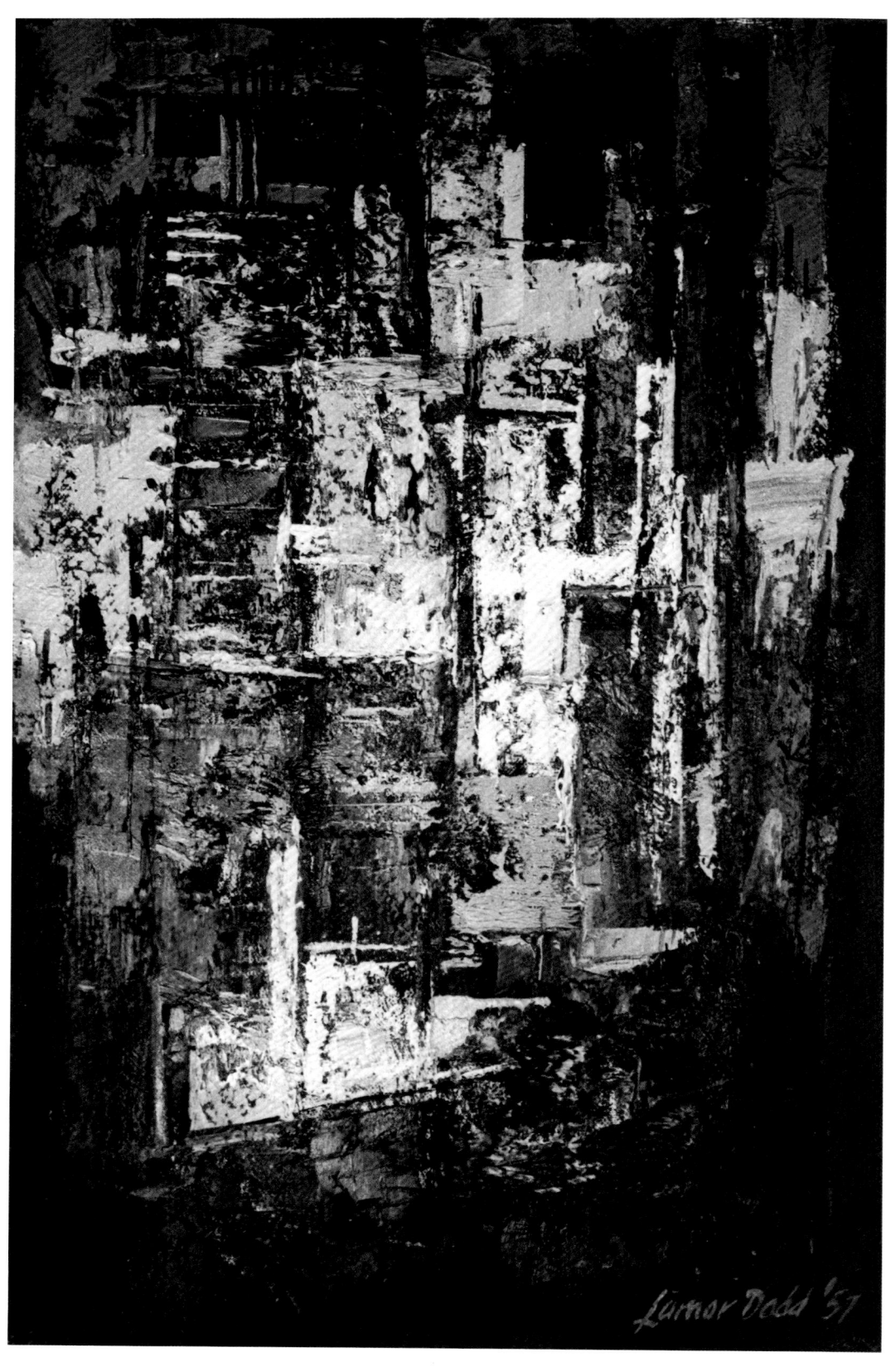

Lamar Dodd '57

62. European Hillside

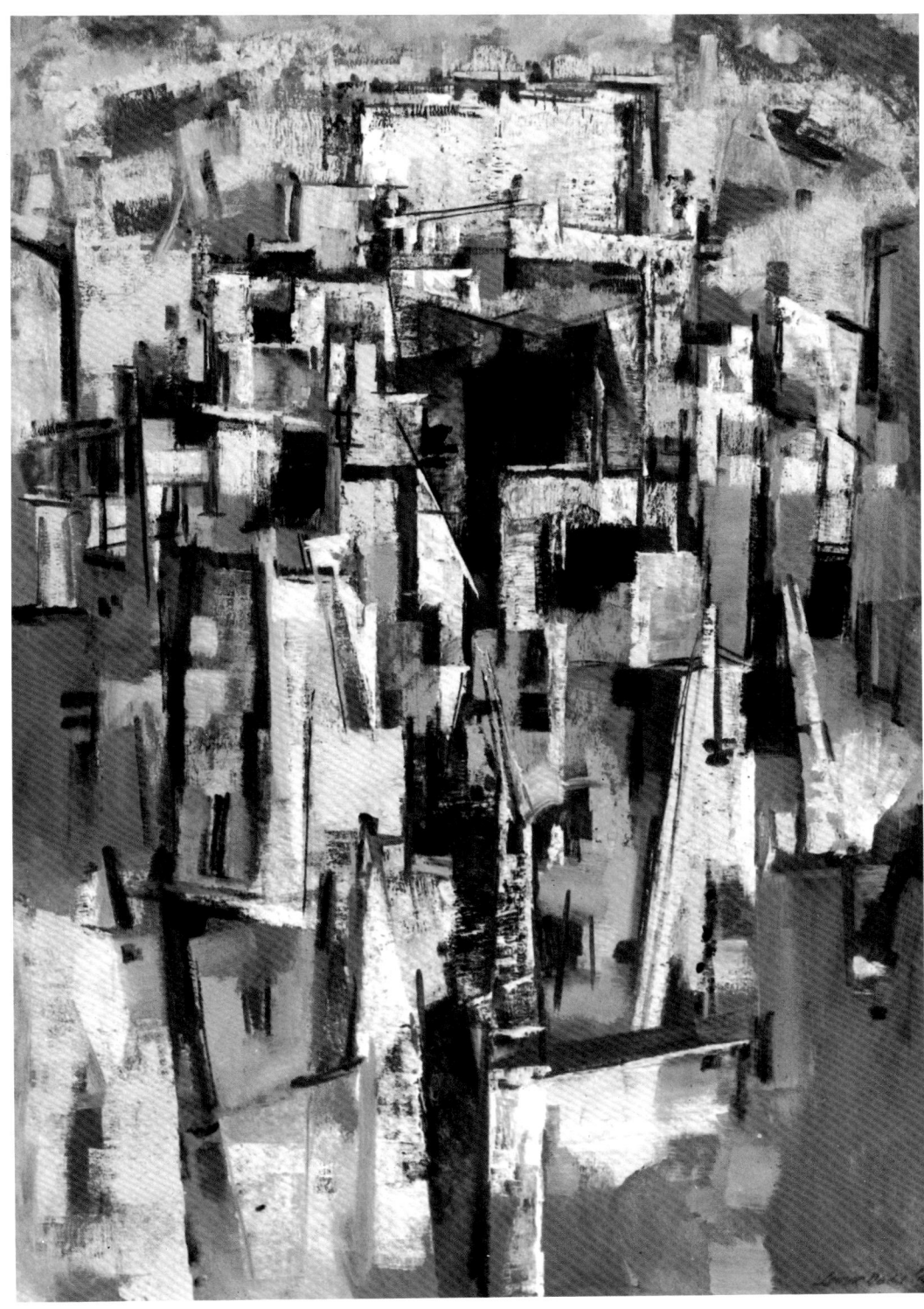

75

66. Aurangabad Market

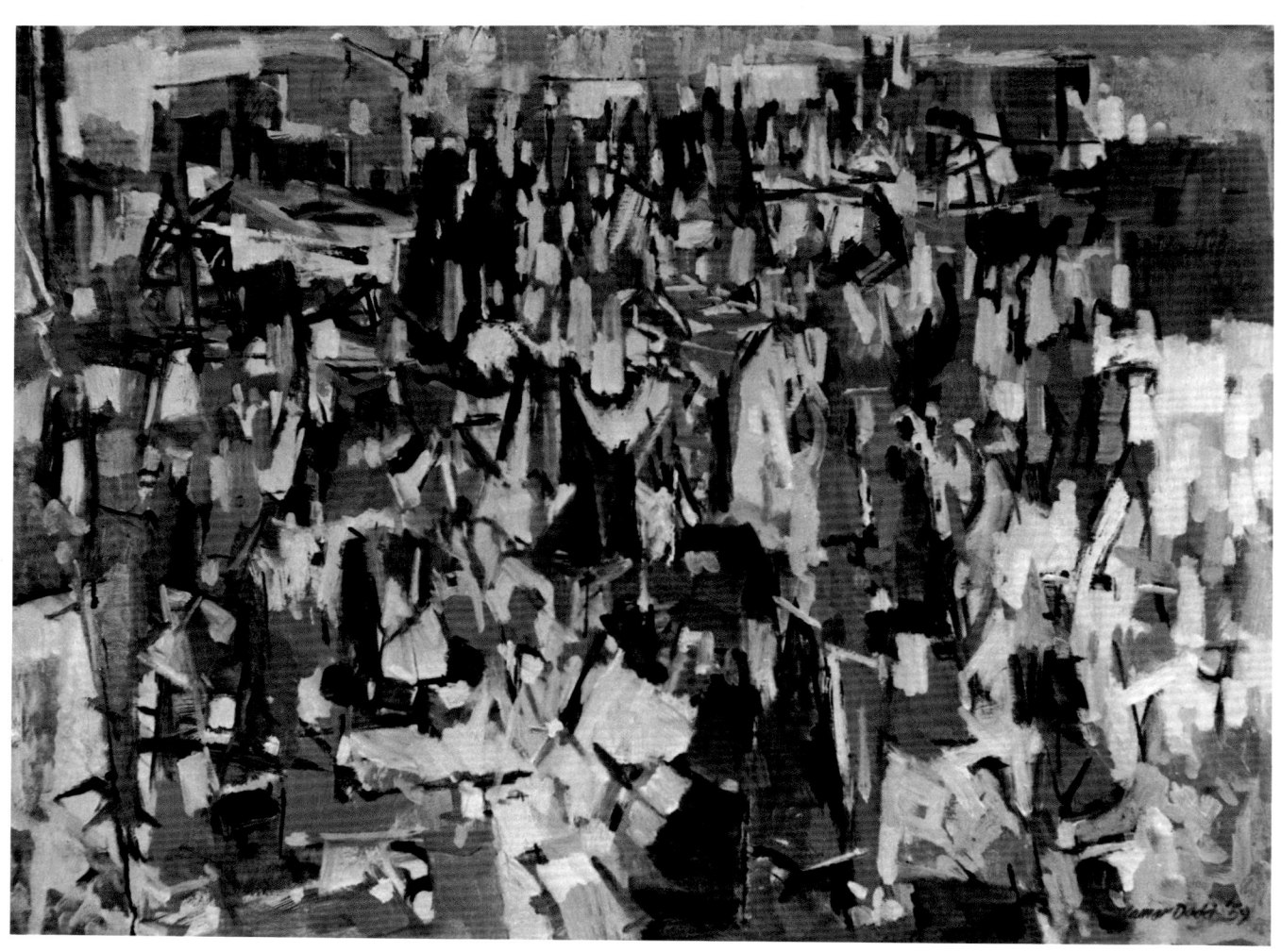

68. Toledo

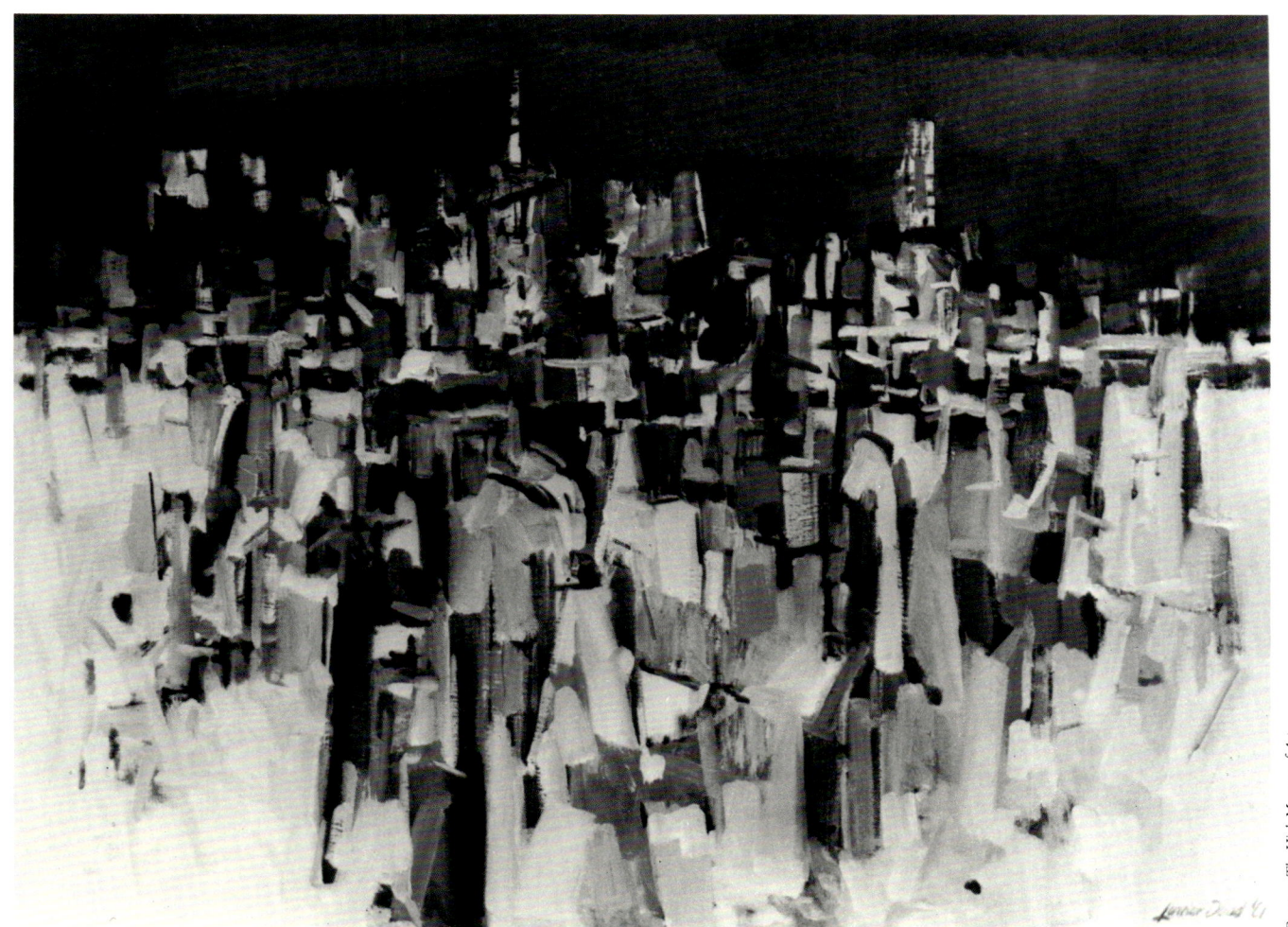

Toledo

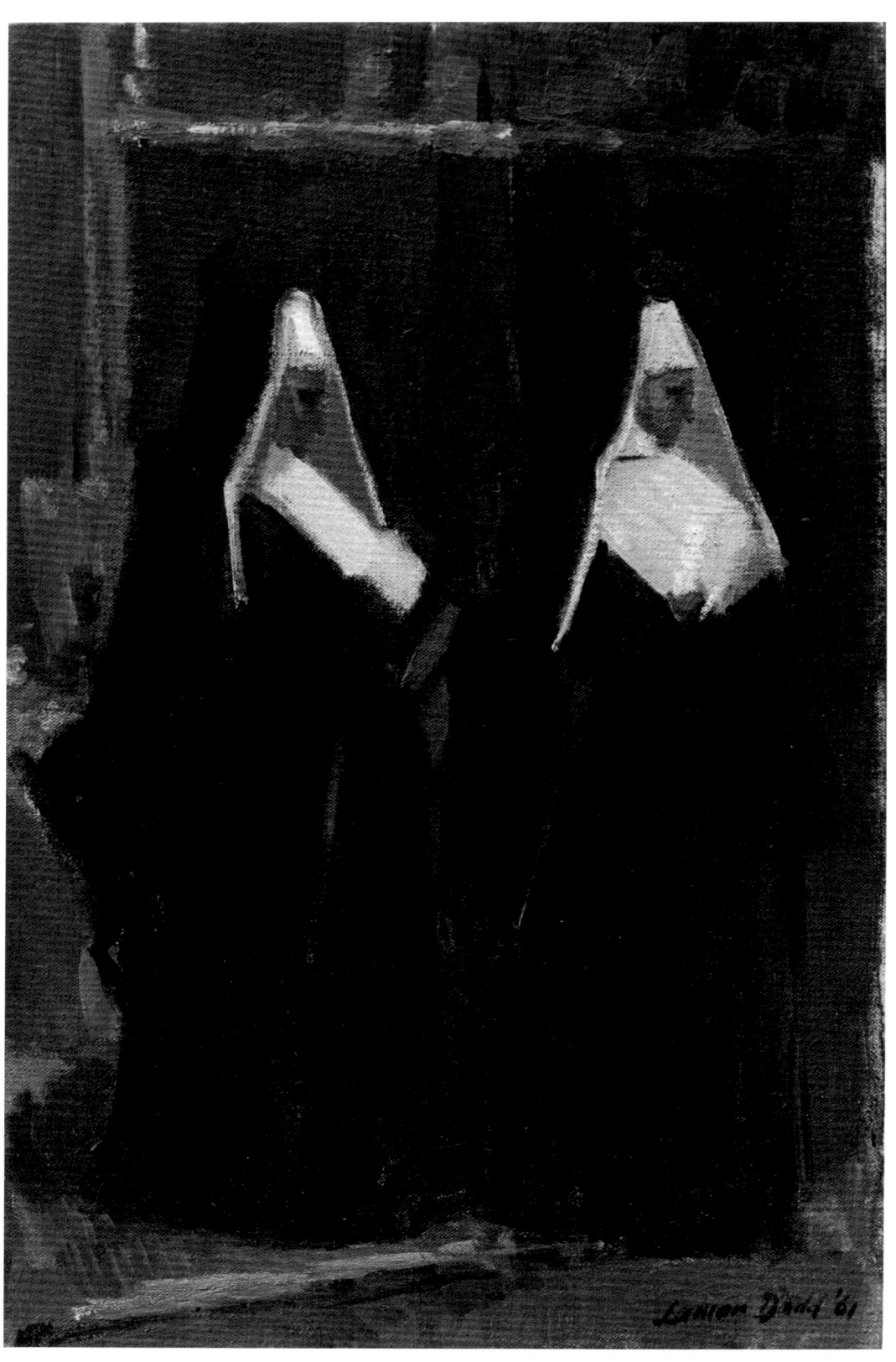

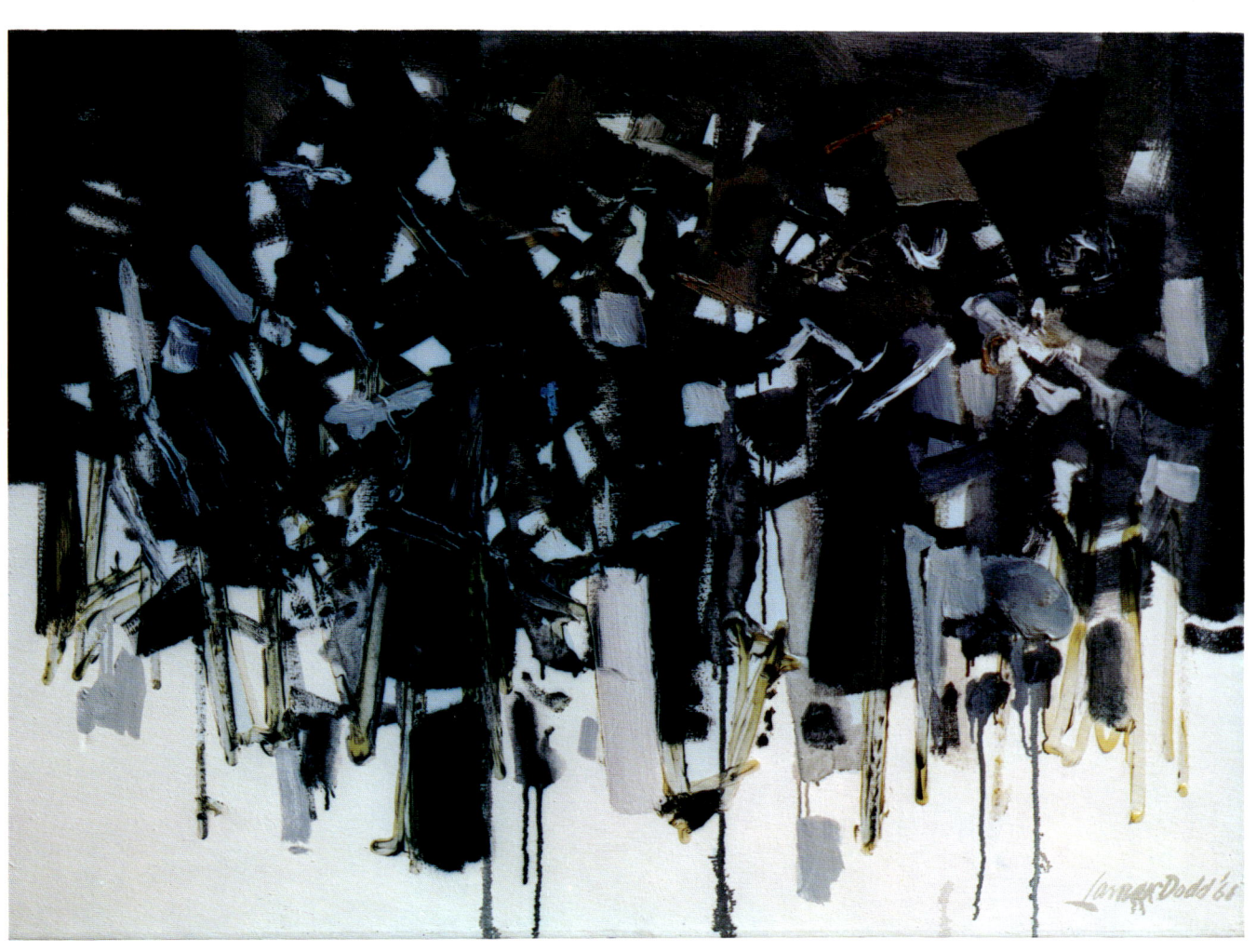

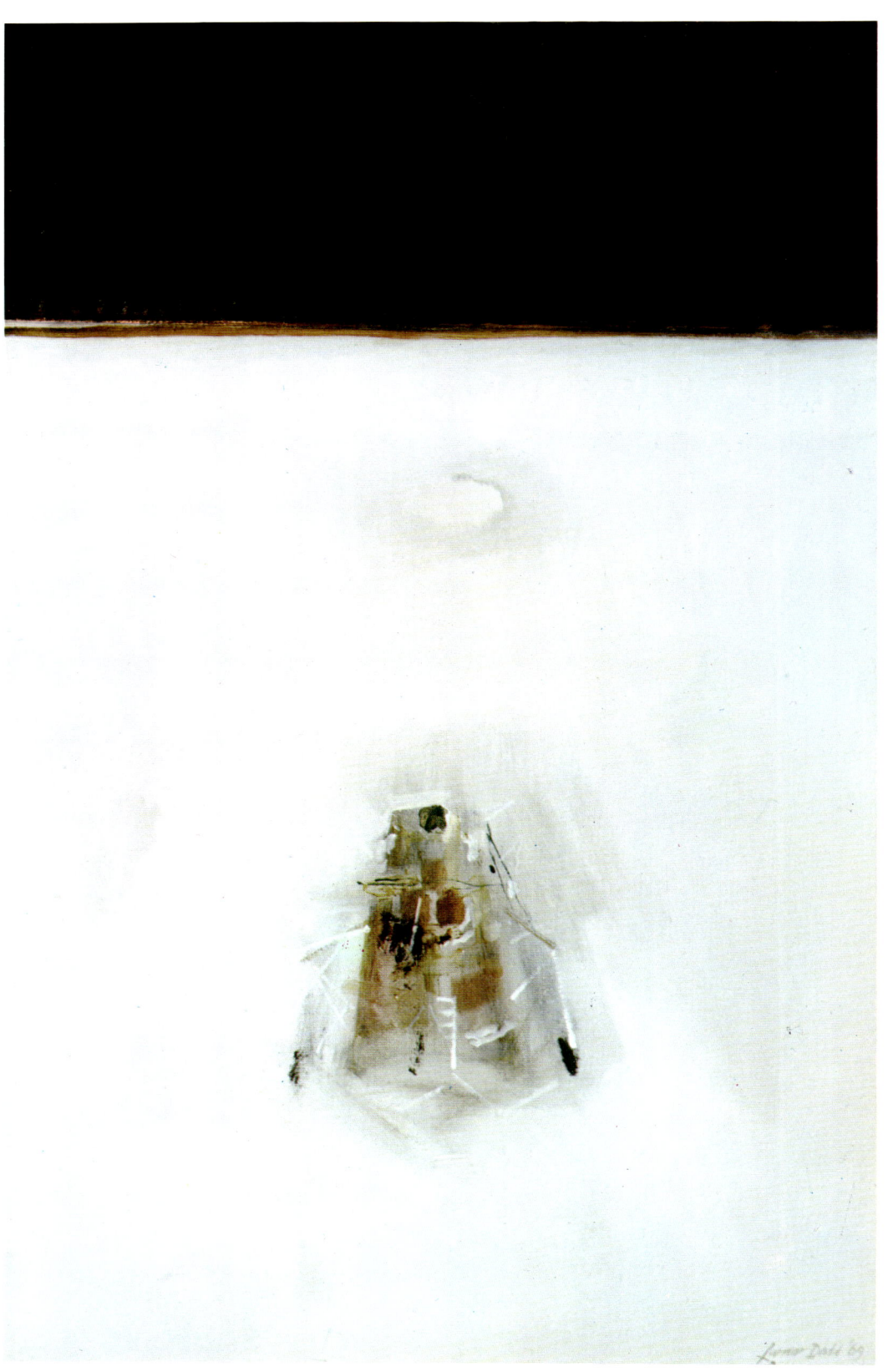

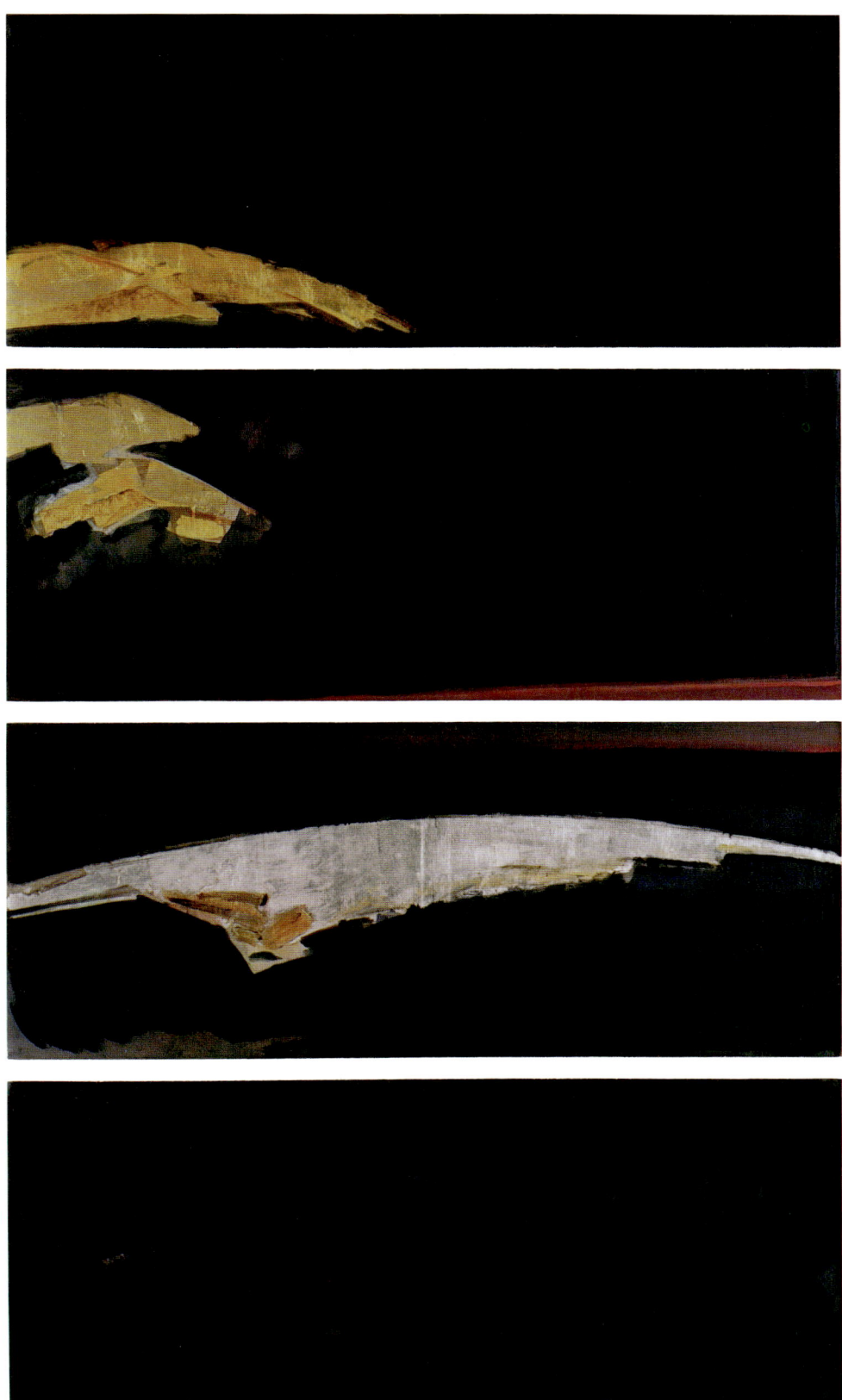

90. Watch at Night (Night before Launch)

Lent by National Aeronautics and Space Administration

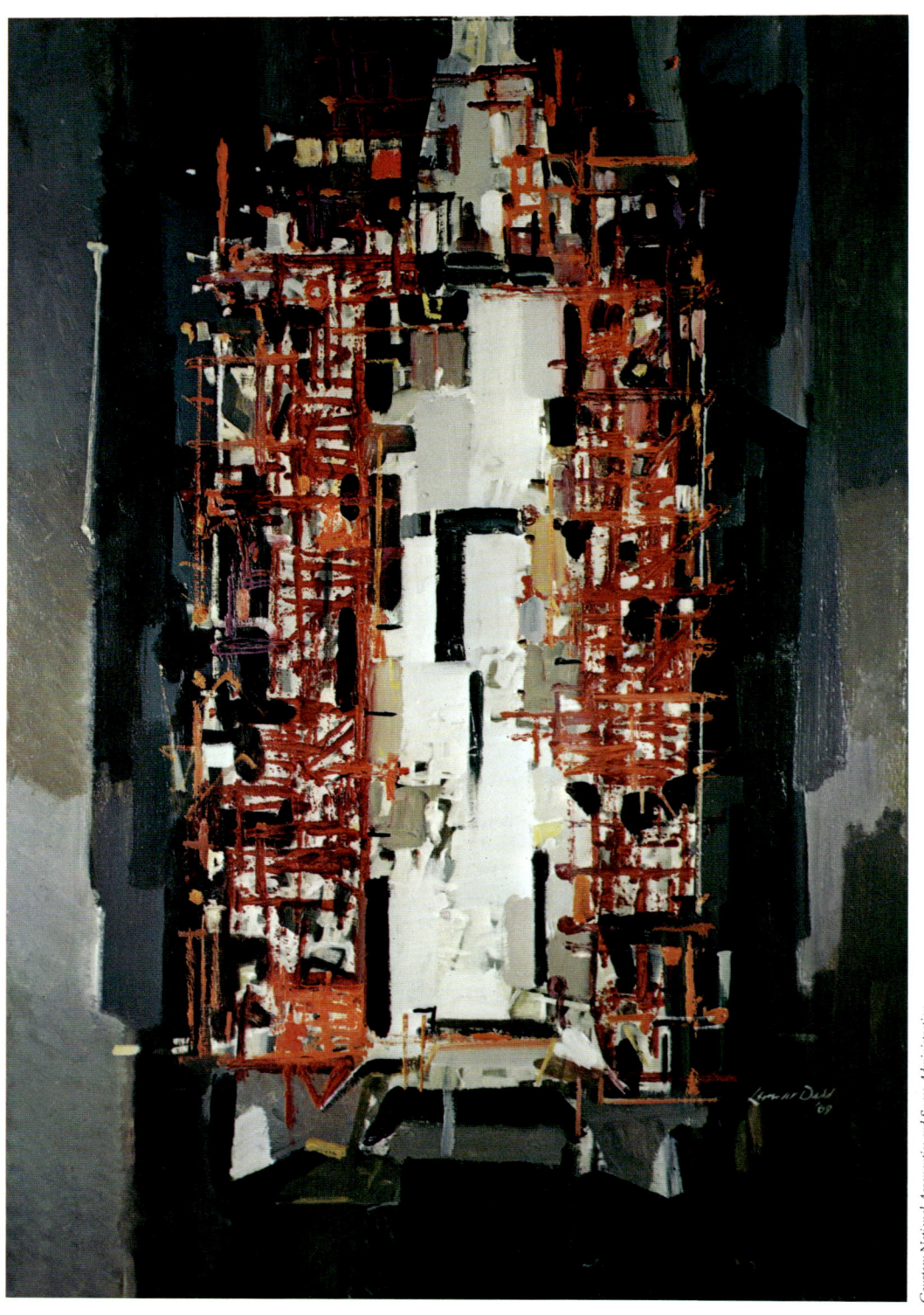

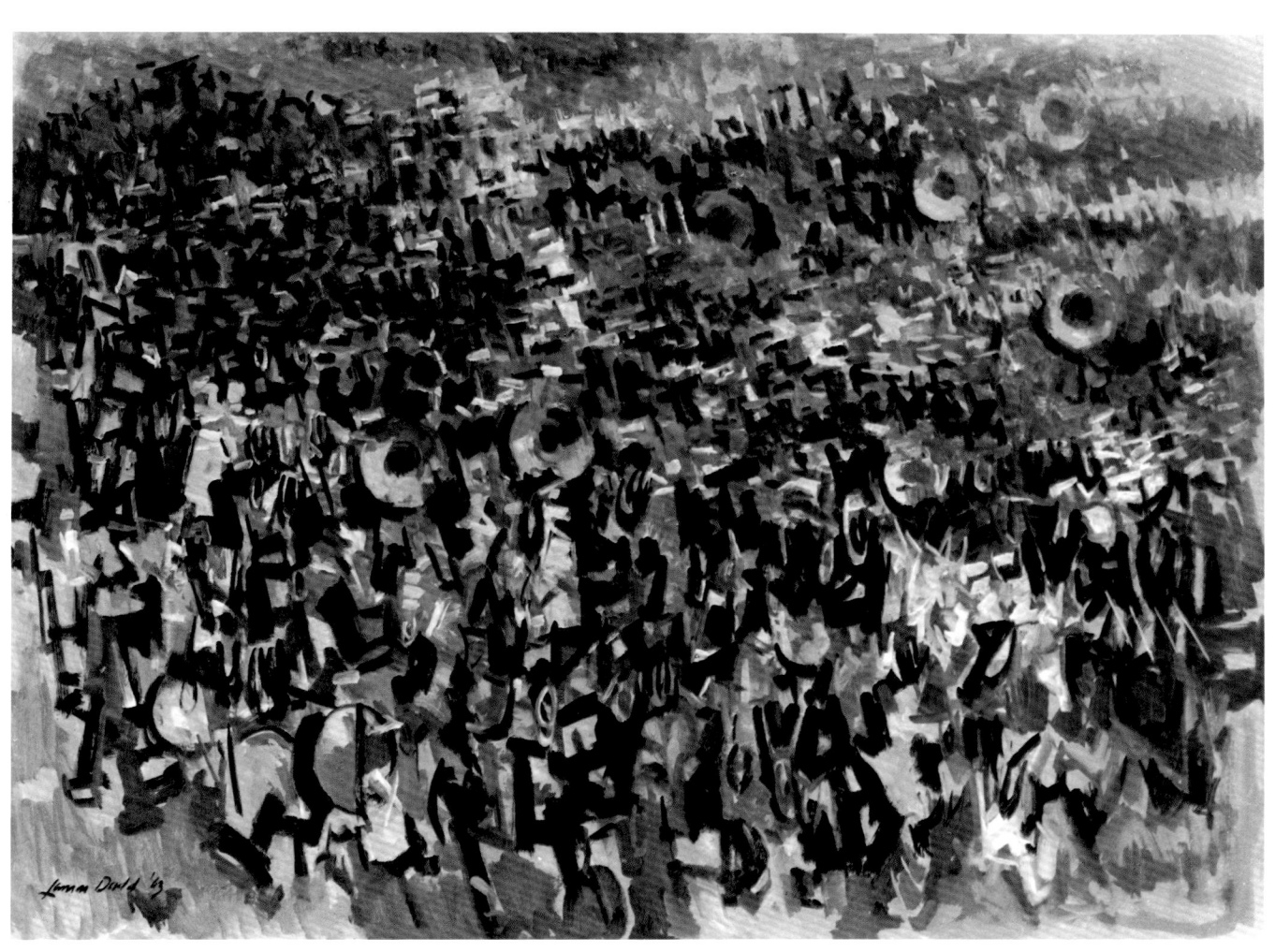

72. The White Room

Lent by National Aeronautics and Space Administration

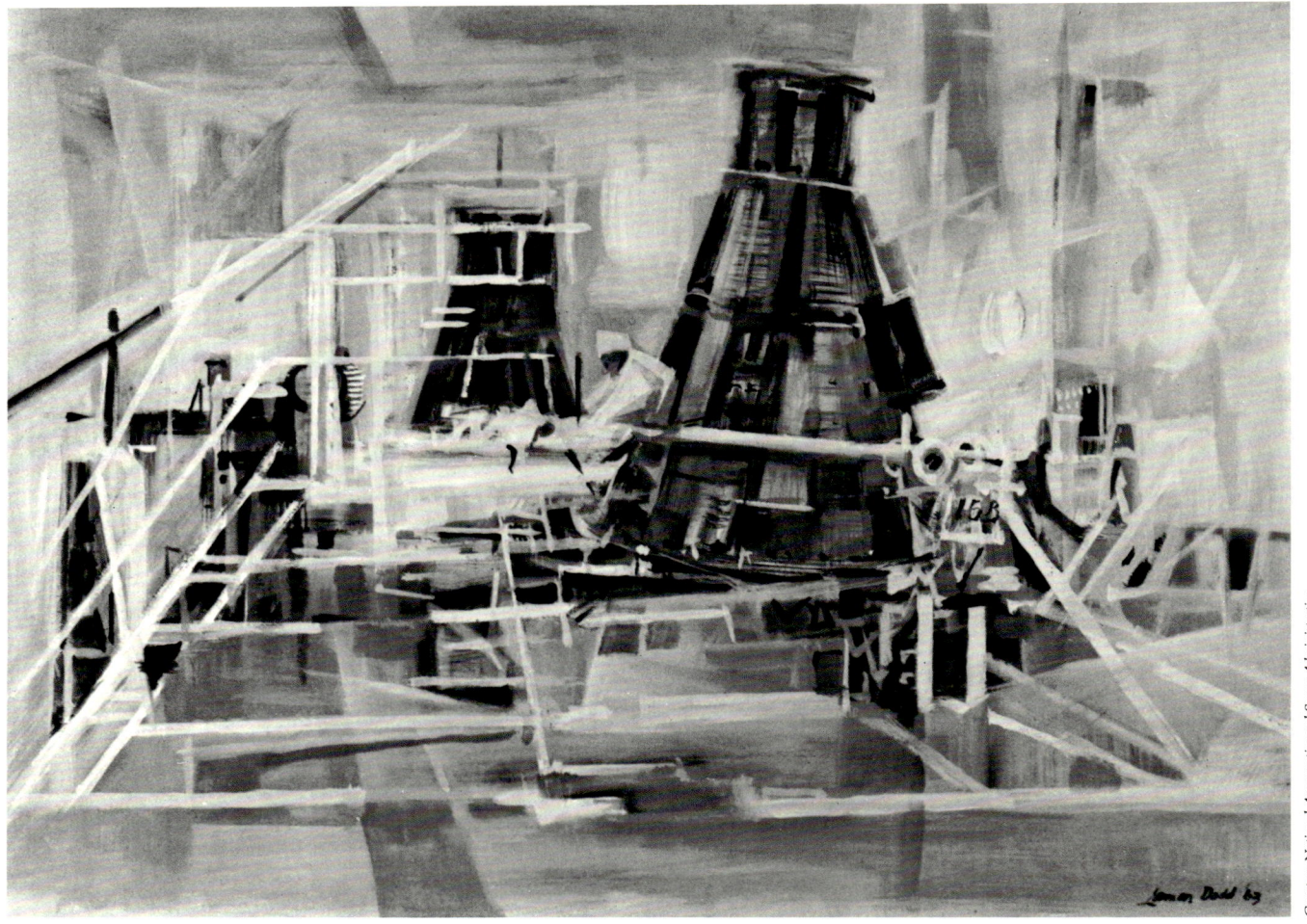

Courtesy National Aeronautics and Space Administration

73. The Cliff
74. The Quiet Sea

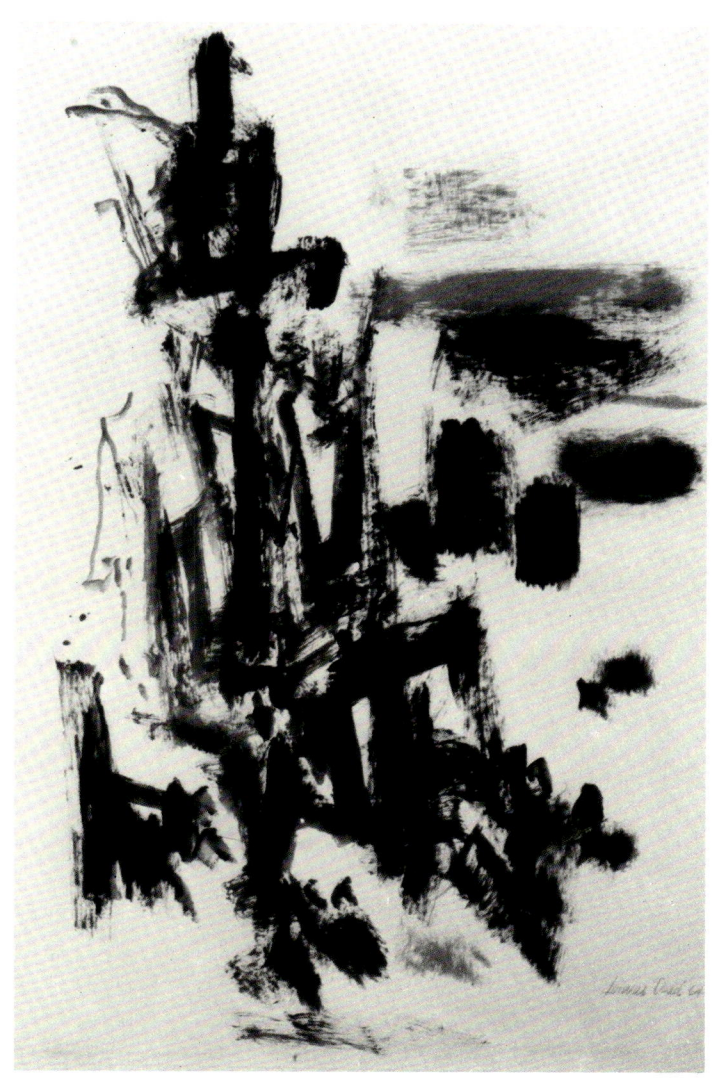

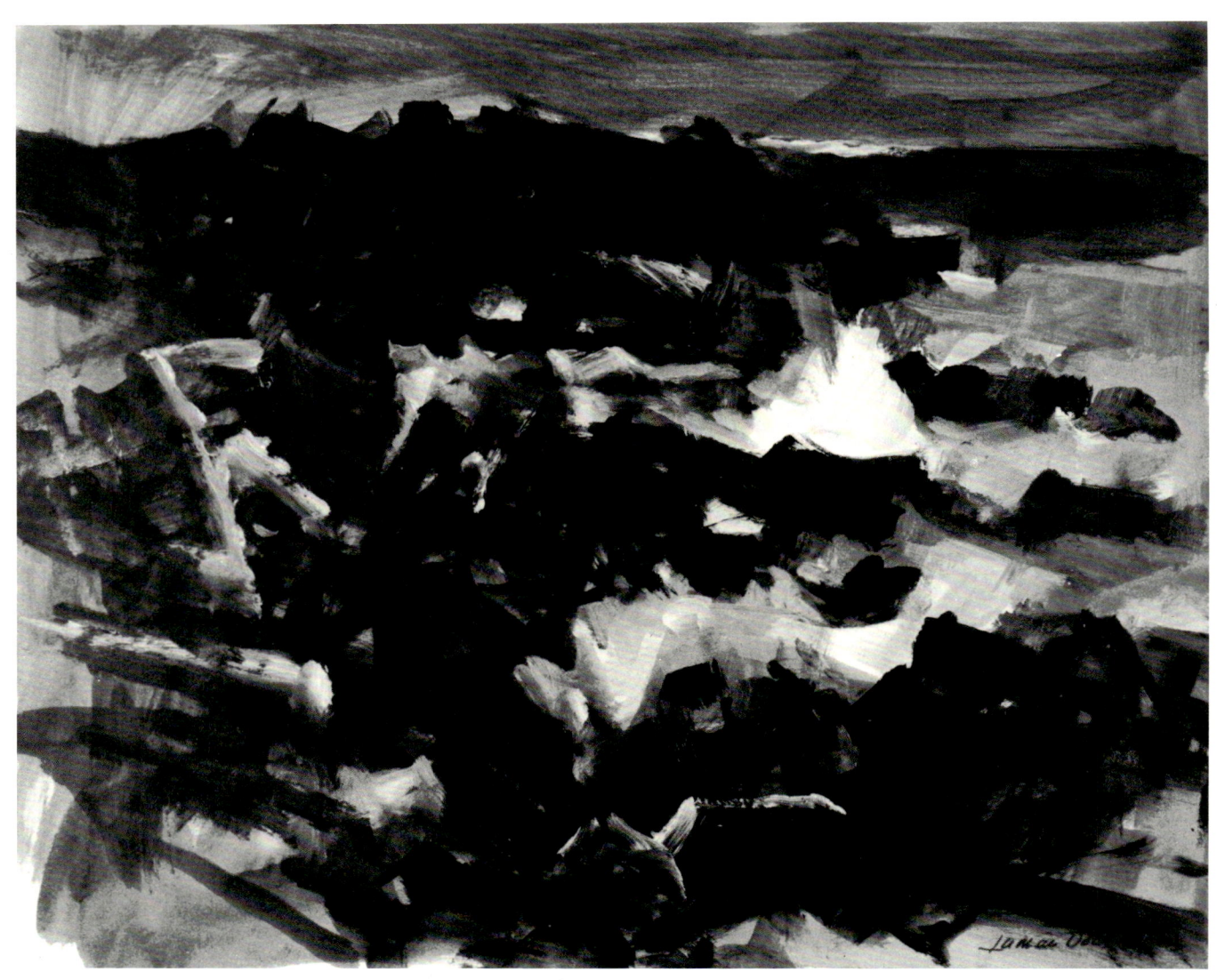

78. Cove Edge

Lent by Grand Central Art Galleries, New York

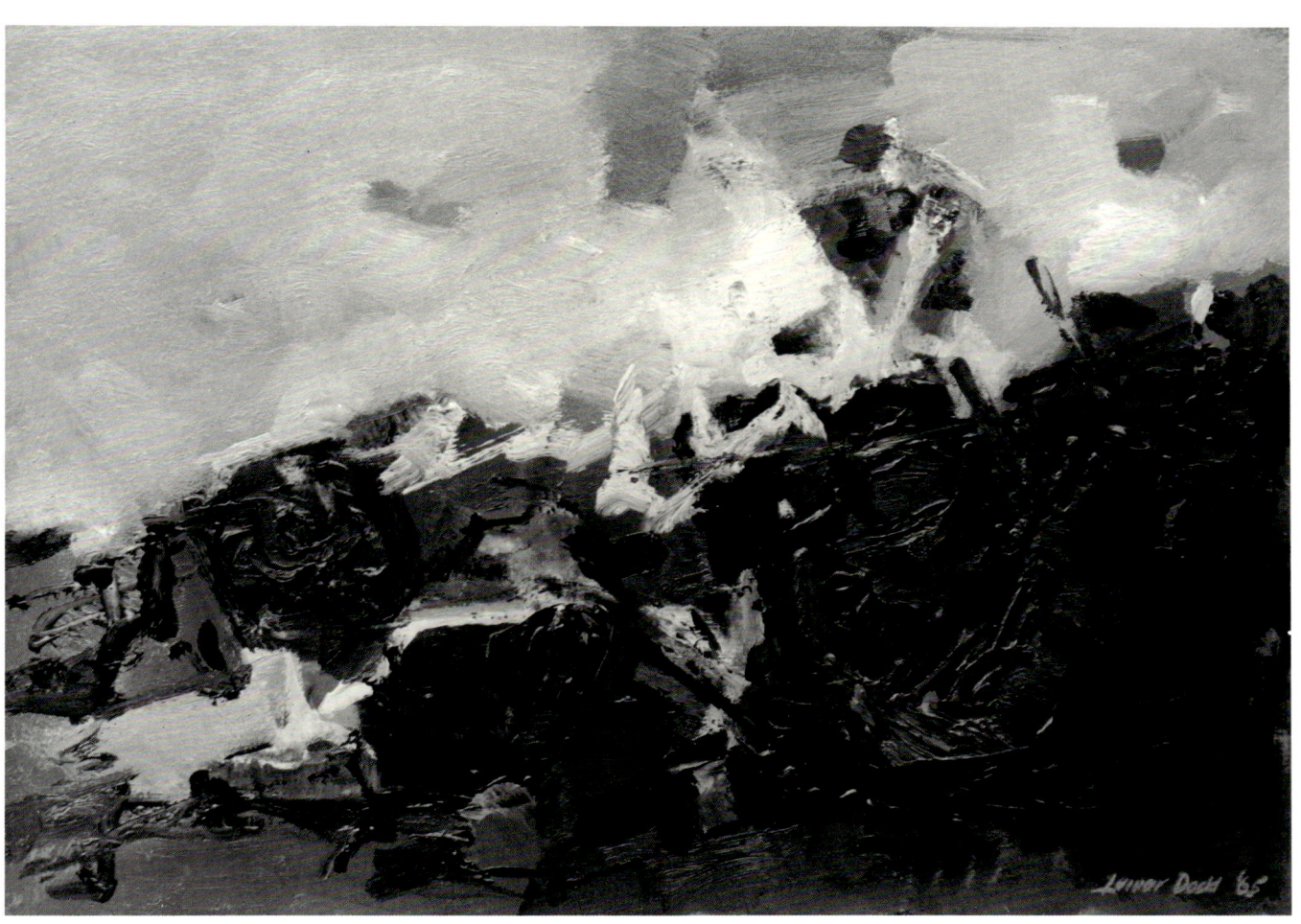

79. Monhegan's Energy

Lent by Grand Central Art Galleries, New York

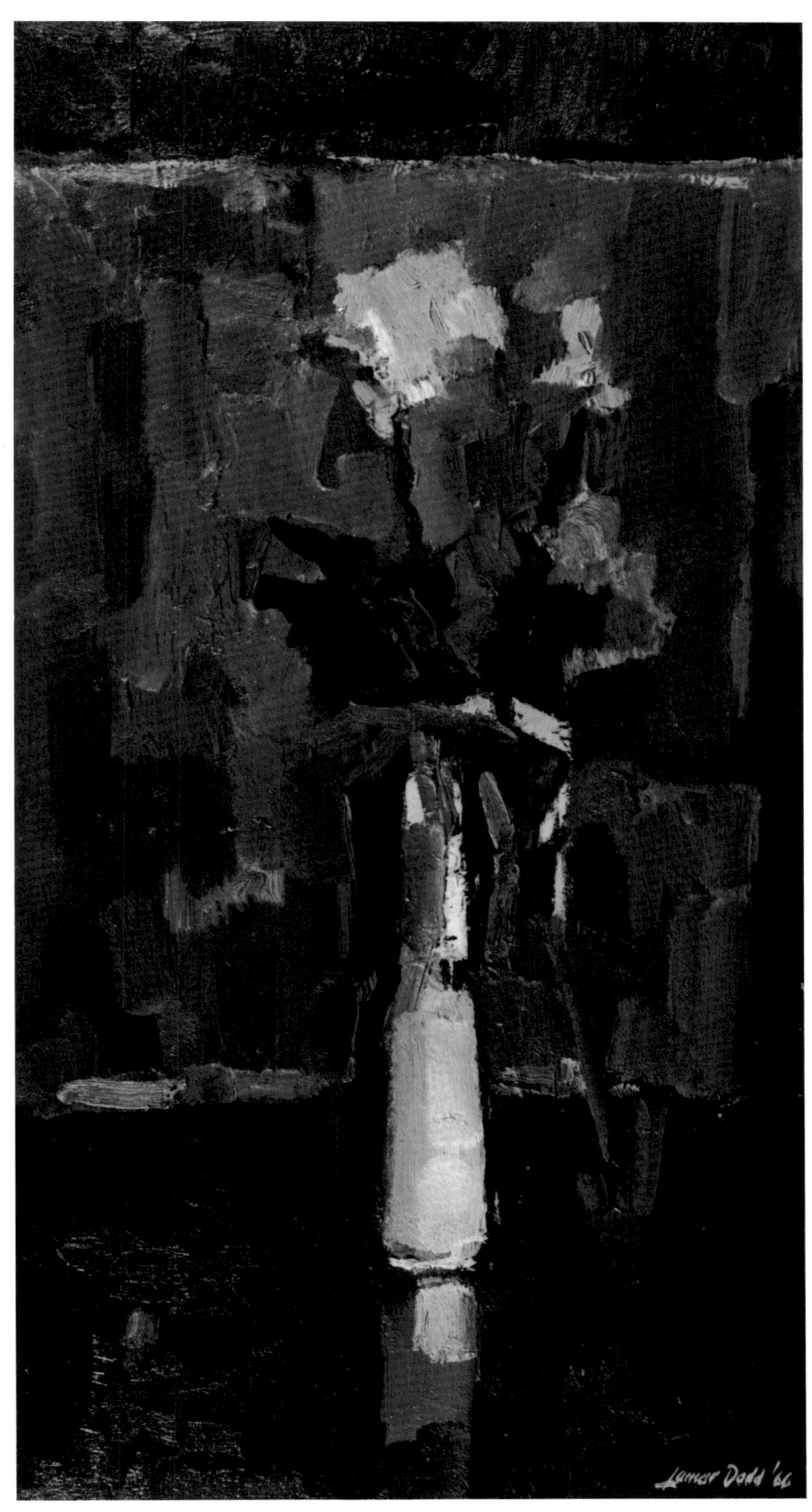

81. Flowers

82. Cityscape 'A'

Lent by Grand Central Art Galleries, New York

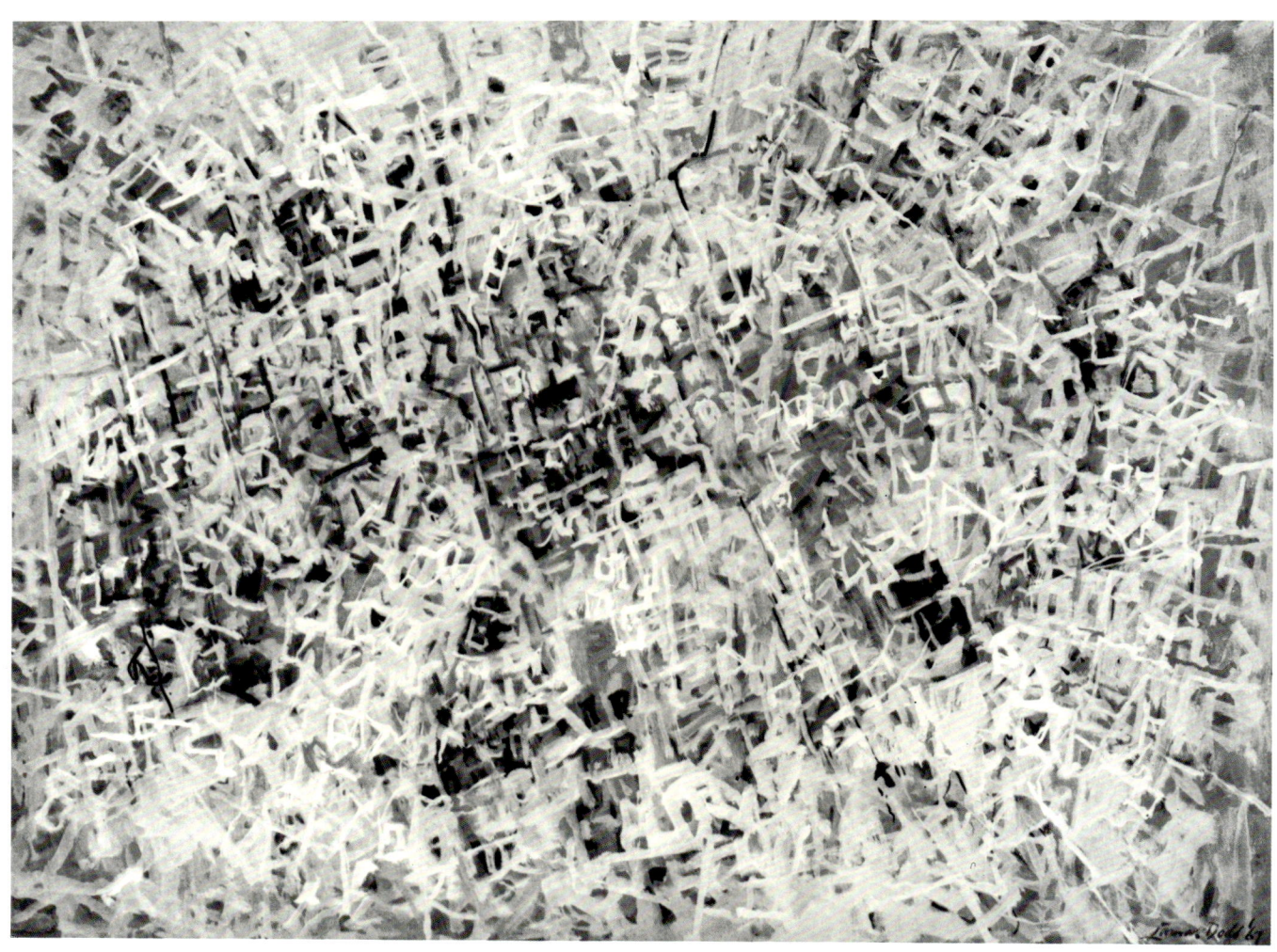

90

Lent by the Addison Gallery of American Art, Phillips Academy, Andover, Massachusetts

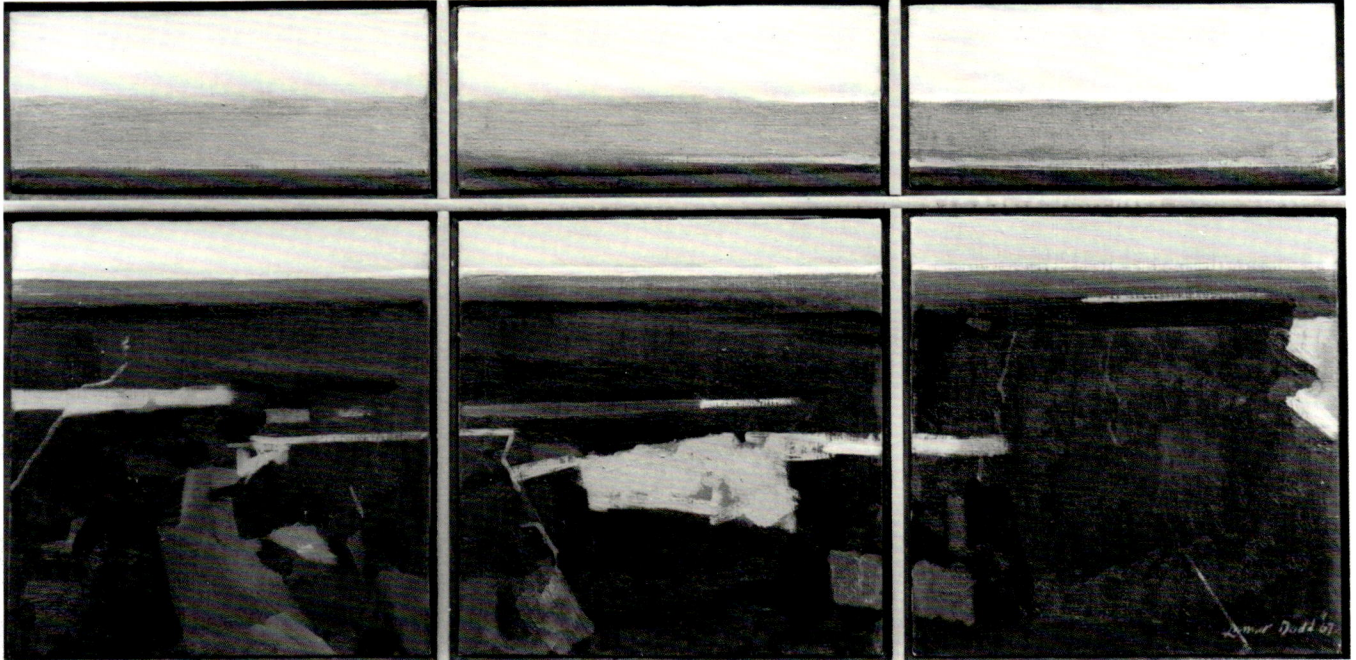

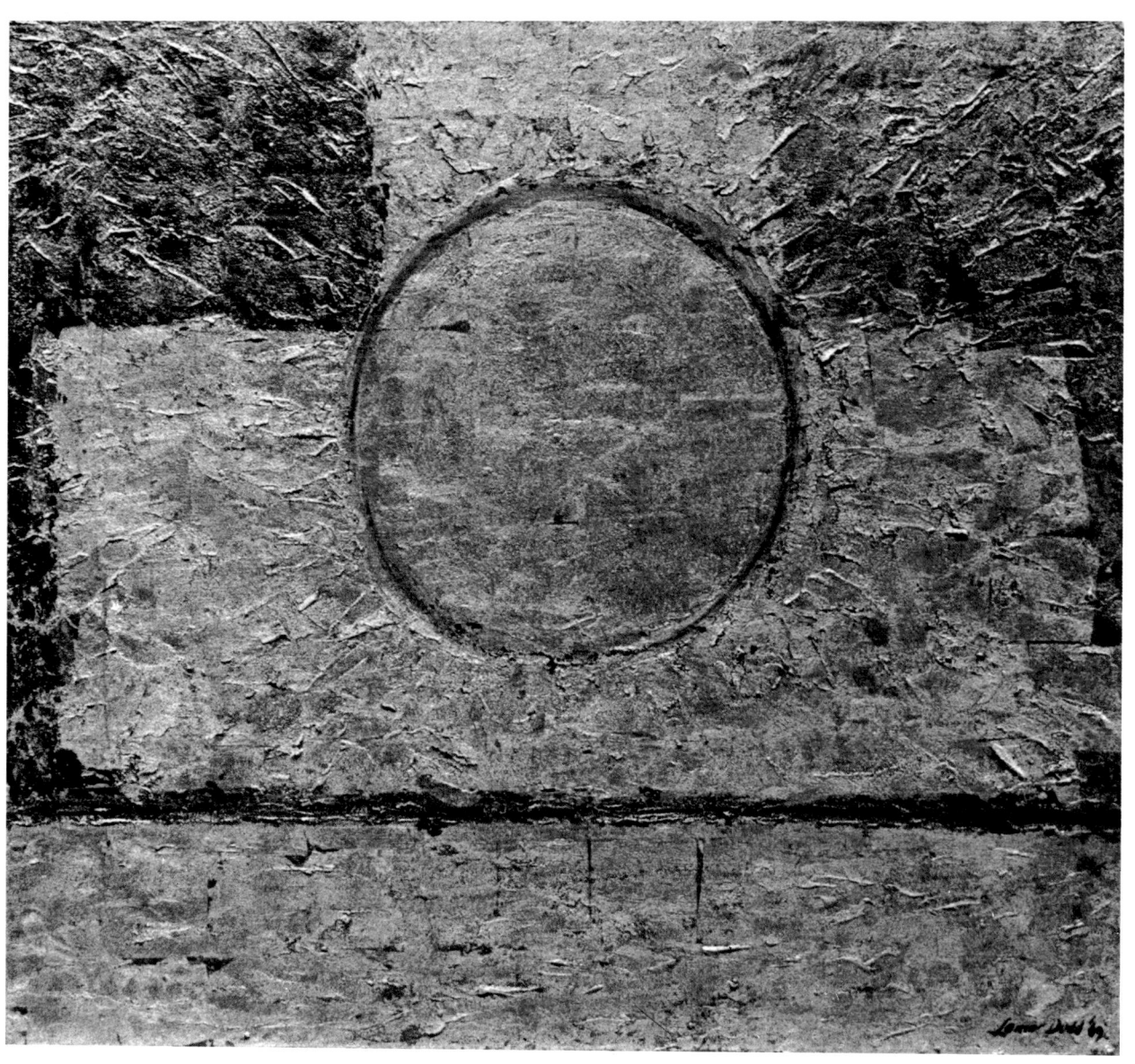

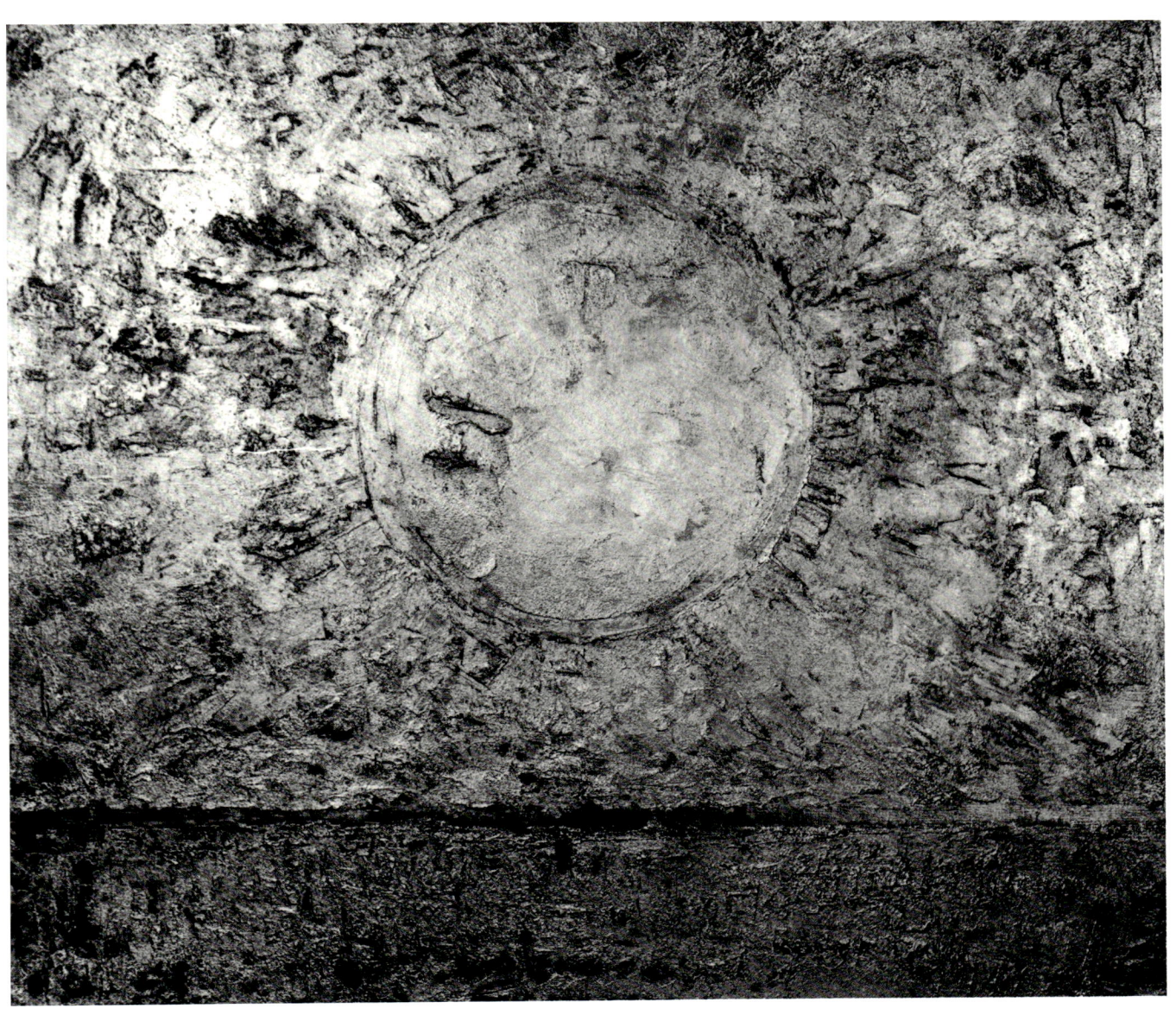

Cosmic Force #2

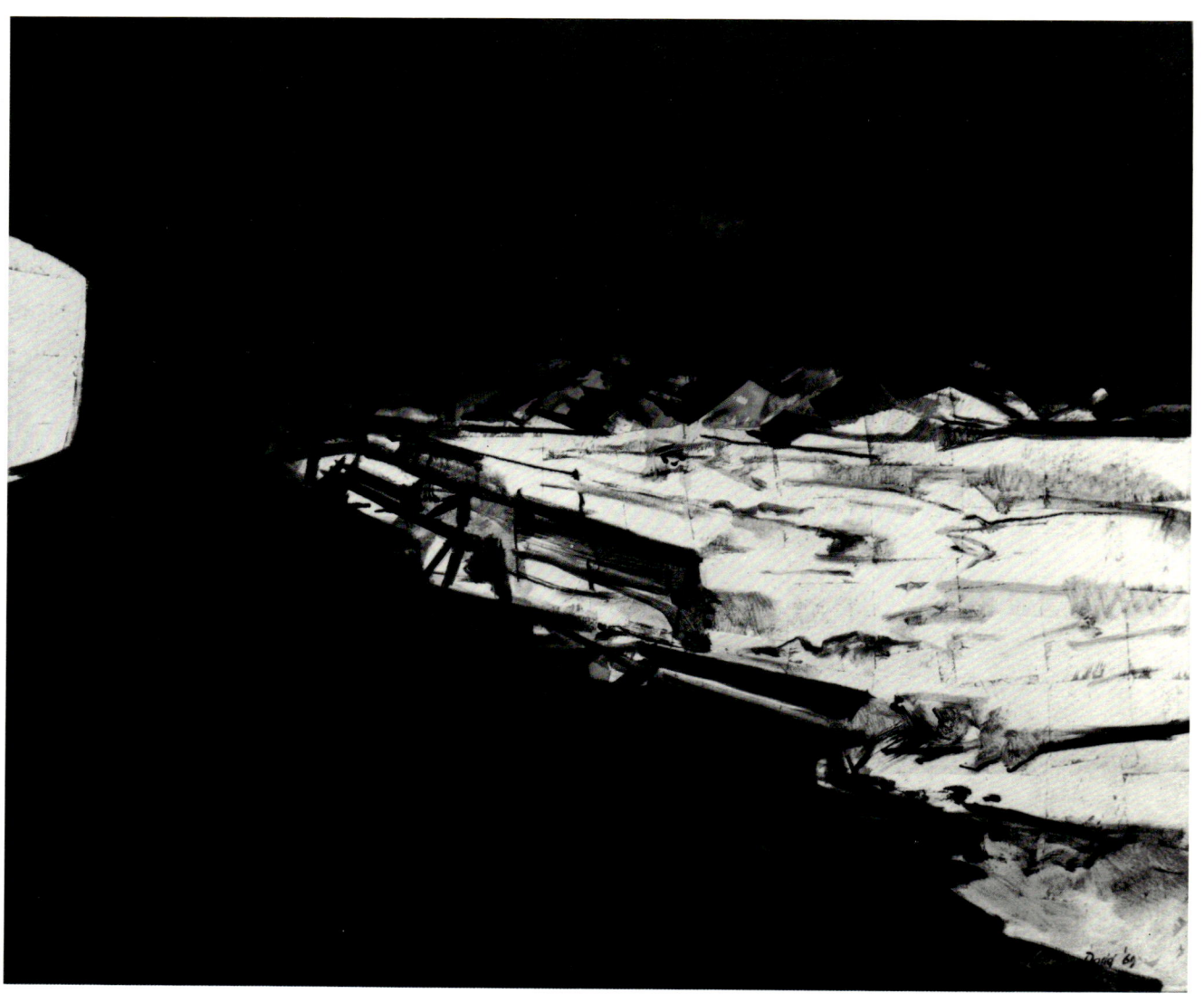

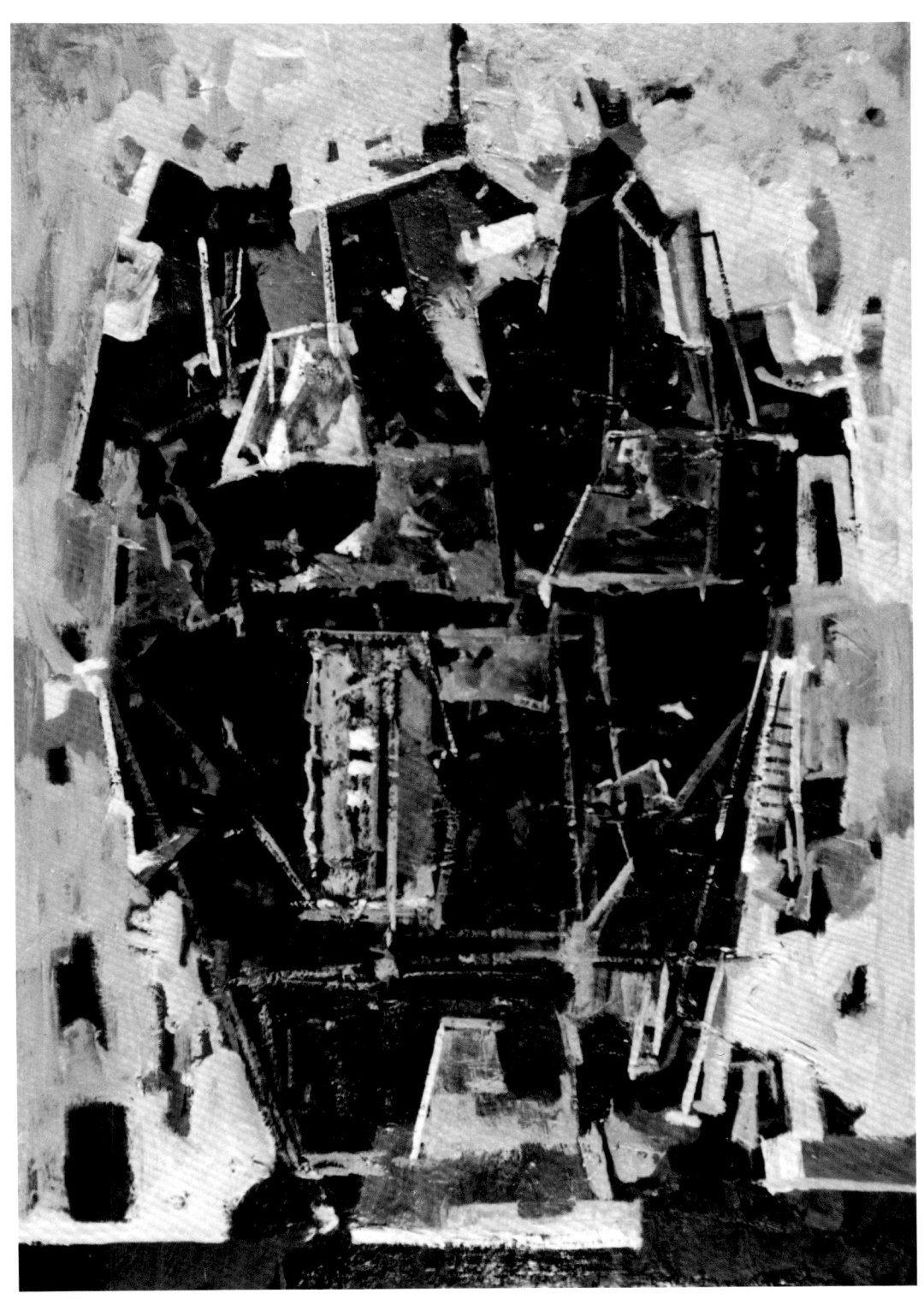

91. The White L.E.M.

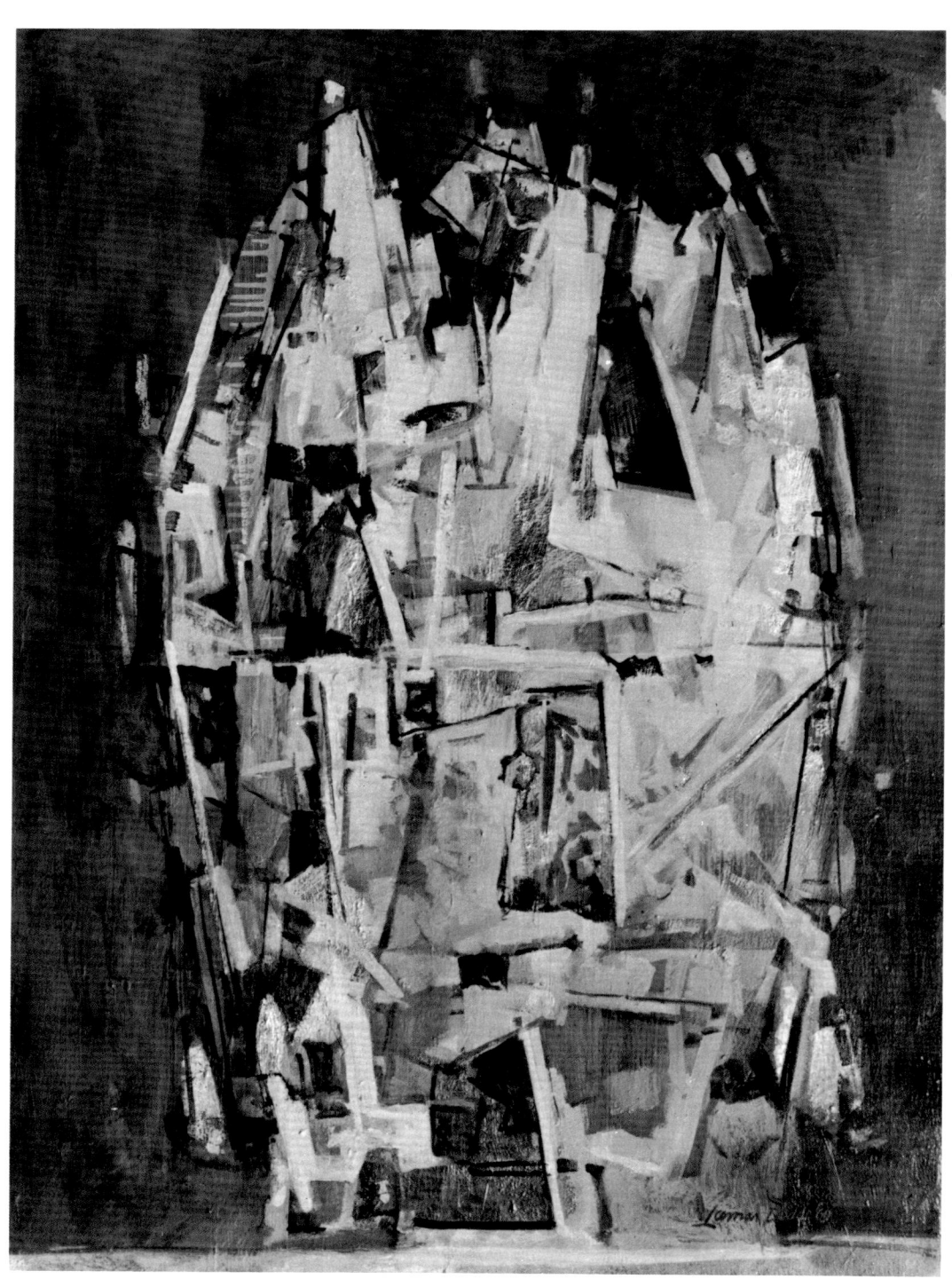

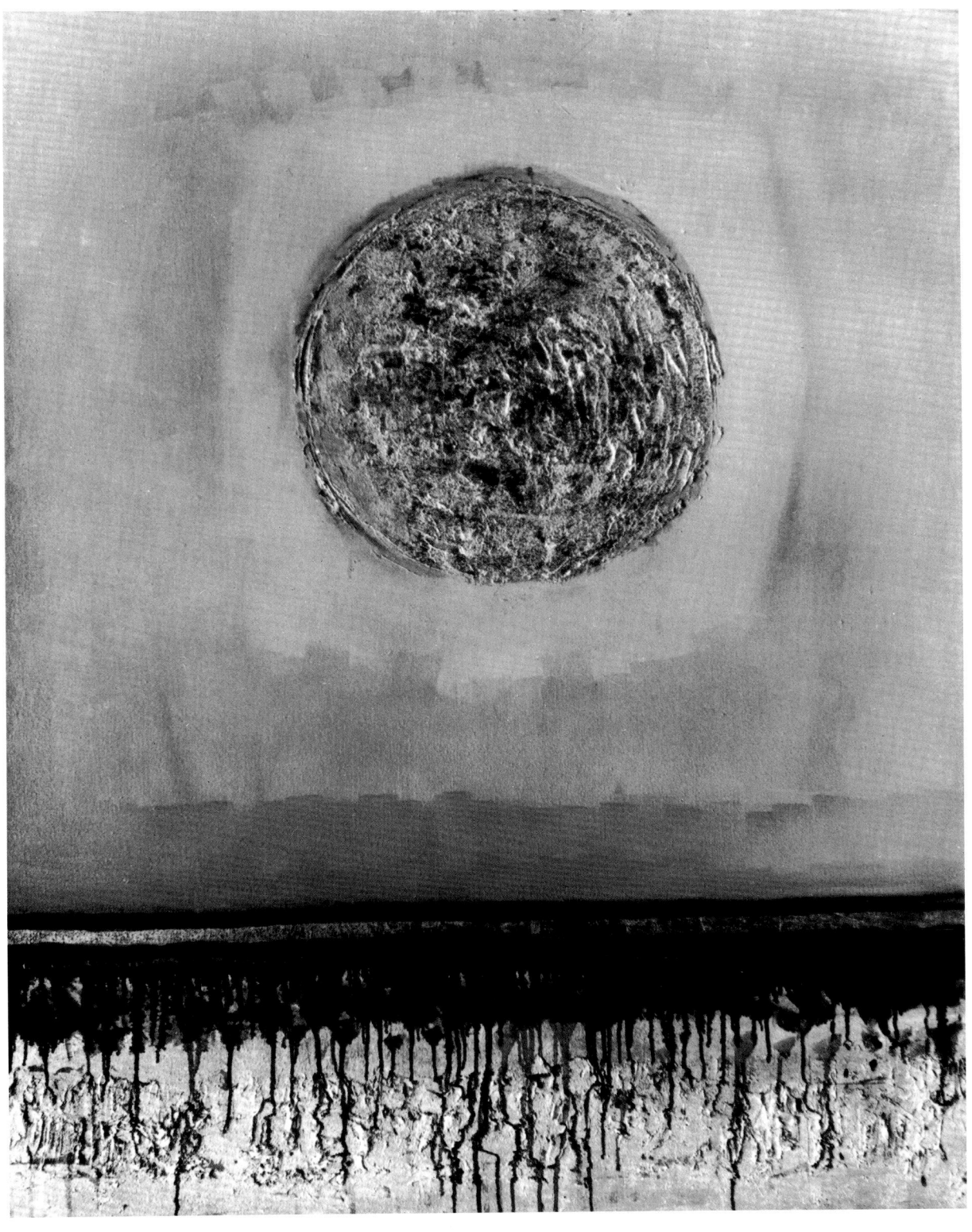

A Statement

Robert D. Calkins
Former Director of
The General Education Board
now, Vice Chancellor—
Social Studies, University of
California—Santa Cruz

Those in philanthropy are occasionally blessed with a few good decisions, troubled by some bad ones, and uninspired by many that result in neither failure nor notable success. It was my privilege as Director of the General Education Board to propose a grant to Lamar Dodd that was followed with those far-reaching ripples of effect for which one always hopes.

I had visited the University of Georgia, met Lamar, and seen something of the energy and promise of the Art Department as he envisioned it. But how to help remained unclear. About that time, James J. Sweeney, then with the Museum of Modern Art in New York City, returned from a lecture assignment at the University of Georgia. I invited him for a luncheon at which we discussed the prospects in Lamar's department. Mr. Sweeney agreed that the need was to broaden horizons, and see more of what was going on in art. My suggestion that Lamar be sent on a trip to Europe seemed to both of us a promising way to begin. An hour later I called Lamar by telephone and assured him of our support if he would go on such a trip. He readily agreed.

He spent a few months first visiting art centers in this country. Then, off to Europe he went. Only he could describe the effect this experience had on his painting and his conceptions for his department. But both were transformed in that mysterious way no other person can explain. This volume, however, is testimony of the effect.

Lamar's painting took on the quest for new styles, new interests, new subjects, and new manners of expression that have been a source of joy to those who have followed his work. The growing number of his exhibitions has attracted the interest of many more.

His department soared to new achievements, also. He assembled a lively staff, acquired a new attractive building for his department, and launched a graduate program of special promise.

Since that first telephone call, I have looked back on the grant to Lamar Dodd as one of the most rewarding and gratifying grants I ever made as a 'philanthropoid.' It was more than chance that the award should have gone to Lamar. But it was Lamar's exceptional abilities and expanding concepts of where he wanted to go that yielded the glorious achievement in both his painting and in his department. His notable achievements are landmarks in art in which we can all rejoice.

The exhibition has been made possible through generous loans from the following:

Dr. and Mrs. Morris B. Abram
Mr. and Mrs. Philip H. Alston, Jr.
Mr. and Mrs. William J. Cabin
Dr. and Mrs. Fred C. Davison
Miss Irene Dodd
Mrs. John S. Dodd, Sr.
Mr. and Mrs. Lamar Dodd
Mr. and Mrs. George W. Funderburk, Jr.
Dr. and Mrs. John E. Imbody
Mr. and Mrs. W. Porter Kellam
Miss Barbara Stanwyck

Addison Gallery of American Art
Columbus Gallery of Arts and Crafts
Cranbrook Museum of Art
Georgia Museum of Art, The University of Georgia
Grand Central Art Galleries
Grand Rapids Art Museum
The High Museum of Art
Lehigh University
Memorial Art Gallery of the University of Rochester
The Metropolitan Museum of Art
The Montclair Art Museum
National Aeronautics and Space Administration
Pennsylvania Academy of the Fine Arts
Sheldon Memorial Art Gallery, The University of Nebraska
Virginia Museum of Fine Arts
Whitney Museum of American Art

Catalogue of the Exhibition

Notes on the Catalogue:
The arrangement is chronological.
Measurements are in inches, height preceding width.
All works are from the artist's collection
unless otherwise noted.

1. Manhattan Bridge, Bowery
    1929, oil on canvas
    26 x 32, signed lower right
    [Plate, page 23]

2. Still Life with Apples
    1929, oil on canvas
    20 x 24, signed lower right
    [Color plate, page 19]

3. Excavation for Empire State Building
    1930, oil on canvas
    30 x 24, signed lower right
    [Plate, page 24]

4. Empress of Britain
    1931, India ink on scratchboard
    10½ x 2¾ (sight size), initialled lower left
    [Plate, page 25]

5. Johnny
    1932, oil on canvas
    18 x 13, signed lower right
    [Plate, page 26]

6. Manhattan
    1932, watercolor on paper
    13⅞ x 18¼ (sight size), signed and
    dated lower right
    [Plate, page 27]

7. Watermelon Wagon
    1932, watercolor on paper
    13½ x 17½ (sight size), signed lower right

8. Woman in the Window
    1932, watercolor on paper
    18 x 25 (sight size),
    signed and dated lower right center
    [Plate, page 28]

9. The Yellow Skirt
    1936, oil on canvas
    30 x 24, signed and dated lower right
    [Color plate, page 20]

10. Basketball
    1937, oil on canvas
    65 x 30, signed and dated lower right
    [Plate, page 29]

11. Monument, Colorado
    1937, oil on canvas
    24 x 30, signed and dated lower right
    [Plate, page 30]

12. A Rainy Ride
    1937, oil on canvas
    23 x 30, signed and dated lower left
    Lent by the Georgia Museum of Art,
    The University of Georgia
    Gift of Alfred H. Holbrook
    [Plate, page 31]

13. Copperhill
    1938, mixed media:
    oil and egg tempera on canvas
    28 x 52, signed and dated lower right
    [Plate, page 32]

14. My Caddy
    1938, mixed media:
    oil and egg tempera on canvas
    34 x 22, signed lower right

15. Rella
    1938, mixed media (egg emulsion) oil
    33 x 24, signed and dated lower left
    [Plate, page 33]

16. Still Life with Self-Portrait
    1938, mixed media:
    oil and egg tempera on canvas
    40 x 30, signed and dated lower right
    [Plate, page 34]

17. View of Athens
    1939, oil on canvas
    30 x 40, signed and dated lower right
    Lent by Dr. and Mrs. Fred C. Davison
    [Plate, page 35]

18. Dew-Ag Hill
    1941, oil on canvas
    24 x 46, signed lower right
    [Plate, page 36]

19. California House
    1942, watercolor on paper
    16 x 23 (sight size), signed lower left
    [Plate, page 37]

20. Skyward
    1944, oil on canvas
    30 x 40, signed and dated lower right
    [Plate, page 38]

21. Still Life with Bottles
    1944, oil on canvas
    24 x 40, signed and dated upper left
    [Plate, page 43]

22. Winter Valley
    1944, oil on canvas
    38 x 50, signed and dated lower left
    [Color plate, page 21]

23. Cotton Pickers
    1945, oil on canvas
    16 x 24, signed lower right
    [Color plate, page 22]

24. From This Earth
    1945, oil on canvas
    24 x 40, signed and dated lower right
    *Lent by Memorial Art Gallery of
    the University of Rochester,
    Rochester, New York,
    Marion Stratton Gould Fund*
    [Plate, page 44]

25. The Breaker
    1946, oil on canvas
    24 x 36, signed and dated lower right
    Lent by Galleries—Cranbrook Academy of Art
    [Plate, page 45]

26. Lumpkin Street
    1946, oil on canvas
    30 x 20, signed and dated lower right
    Lent by Miss Barbara Stanwyck
    [Plate, page 46]

27. Savannah
    1946, oil on canvas
    20 x 30, signed and dated lower right
    *Lent by The Montclair Art Museum,
    Montclair, New Jersey*
    [Plate, page 47]

28. Black Top Table
    1947, oil on canvas
    24 x 36, signed and dated left above center
    [Color plate, page 39]

29. Into the Night
    1947, oil on canvas
    24 x 40, signed and dated lower right
    [Plate, page 48]

30. Objects on the Table
    1947, oil on canvas
    24 x 40, signed and dated lower right
    Lent by Mr. and Mrs. George W. Funderburk, Jr.
    [Plate, page 49]

31. Solitude
    1947, oil on canvas
    24 x 36, signed and dated lower left
    [Plate, page 50]

48. Buoys, Monhegan
   1955, watercolor on paper
   26 x 17⅛ (sight size),
   signed and dated lower right

49. Forms of the Sea
   1955, oil on gesso panel
   6 x 9, signed and dated lower right
   [Color plate, page 59]

50. Gondolas
   1955, oil on canvas
   22 x 40, signed and dated lower right
   [Color plate, page 60]

51. Hilltop Town
   1955, Contè crayon and watercolor on paper
   25⅜ x 17½ (sight size), signed and
   dated vertically, lower right

52. Venetian Patterns
   1955, oil on canvas
   30 x 42, signed and dated lower right
   Lent by Columbus Museum of Arts and Crafts,
   Columbus, Georgia
   [Plate, page 67]

53. White Head
   1955, reed and ink drawing on paper
   13⅞ x 20⅞ (sight size),
   signed and dated lower left
   [Plate, page 68]

54. Cathedral Soliloquy
   1956, oil on canvas
   40 x 20, signed and dated lower right
   Lent by Grand Rapids Art Museum,
   Grand Rapids, Michigan
   [Plate, page 69]

55. Piazza San Marco
   1956, oil on canvas
   30 x 40, signed lower right
   Lent by Mrs. John S. Dodd, Sr.
   [Plate, page 70]

56. St. Mark's Cathedral
   1956, oil on canvas
   16 x 24, signed and dated lower right
   Lent by Mr. and Mrs. William J. Cabin
   [Plate, page 71]

57. They Come, They Go
   1956, oil on canvas
   16 x 36, signed and dated lower right
   Lent by Grand Central Art Galleries, New York
   [Plate, page 72]

58. Across the Bosphorus
   1957, oil on canvas
   30 x 42, signed and dated lower right
   Lent by Pennsylvania Academy of the Fine Arts,
   Philadelphia, Pennsylvania
   [Plate, page 73]

59. Cathedral #1
   1957, oil on canvas
   42 x 20, signed and dated lower right
   Lent by Lehigh University Permanent Collection.
   1958. Ralph Wilson Fund.
   [Color plate, page 61]

60. City
   1957, oil on canvas
   18 x 12, signed and dated lower right
   [Plate, page 74]

61. City at Dusk
   1957, oil on canvas
   24 x 36, signed and dated lower right
   Lent by The High Museum of Art

62. European Hillside
   1957, oil on canvas
   42 x 30, signed and dated lower right
   Lent by Whitney Museum of American Art,
   New York
   [Plate, page 75]

63. The Great City
   1957, oil on canvas
   12 x 18, signed and dated lower right
   Lent by Mr. and Mrs. William J. Cabin

64. Pink Patterns
   1957, watercolor on paper
   18 x 14⅝ (sight size),
   signed and dated lower right

65. The Grand Canal
   1958, oil on canvas
   48 x 28, signed and dated lower right
   [Color plate, page 62]

66. Aurangabad Market
    1959, oil on canvas
    30 x 42, signed and dated lower right
    Lent by Dr. and Mrs. John E. Imbody
    [Plate, page 76]

67. Jaipur No. 2
    1960, oil on canvas
    16 x 38, signed lower right

68. Toledo
    1961, oil on canvas
    30⅛ x 42⅛, signed and dated lower right
    Lent by The High Museum of Art
    [Plate, page 77]

69. Two Nuns
    1961, oil on canvas
    15 x 10, signed and dated lower right
    [Plate, page 78]

70. Bands Day
    1963, oil on canvas
    36 x 50, signed and dated lower left
    [Plate, page 83]

71. The Harbor
    1963, watercolor on paper
    20½ x 28 (sight size),
    signed and dated lower right
    [Color plate, page 59]

72. The White Room
    1963, gouache on paper
    20½ x 29 (sight size),
    signed and dated lower right
    *Lent by National Aeronautics
    and Space Administration*
    [Plate, page 84]

73. The Cliff
    1964, watercolor on paper
    24 x 16½ (sight size),
    signed and dated lower right
    [Plate, page 85]

74. The Quiet Sea
    1964, polymer on paper, mounted on matboard
    7½ x 22¼, signed and dated lower right
    [Plate, page 85]

75. Sea Captain's House
    1964, polymer on paper
    9½ x 13 (sight size),
    signed and dated lower right

76. Storm at Lobster
    1964, polymer on paper
    17½ x 22⅝ (sight size),
    signed and dated lower right
    [Plate, page 86]

77. Cosmography
    1965, oil on canvas
    40 x 44, signed and dated lower right

78. Cove Edge
    1965, oil on canvas
    16 x 24, signed and dated lower right
    Lent by Grand Central Art Galleries, New York
    [Plate, page 87]

79. Monhegan's Energy
    1965, oil on canvas
    28 x 48, signed and dated lower right
    Lent by Grand Central Art Galleries, New York
    [Plate, page 88]

80. After Casals #1
    1966, oil on canvas
    30 x 42, signed and dated lower right
    [Color plate, page 79]

81. Flowers
    1966, oil on canvas
    34 x 18, signed and dated lower right
    [Plate, page 89]

82. Cityscape 'A'
    1967, oil on canvas
    30 x 42, signed and dated lower right
    Lent by Grand Central Art Galleries, New York
    [Plate, page 90]

83. Over and Beyond
    1967, oil on 6 canvases
    17 x 36 (overall size), signed and
    dated lower right, bottom right canvas
    *Lent by Addison Gallery of American Art,
    Phillips Academy, Andover, Massachusetts.*
    [Plate, page 91]

84. Cosmic Force
    1969, oil with silver leaf, on canvas
    36 x 40, signed and dated lower right
    [Plate, page 92]

85. Cosmic Force #2
    1969, oil with silver
    and lemon-gold leaf, on canvas
    40 x 48, signed and dated lower right
    [Color plate, front cover; plate, page 93]

86. Cosmic Landing
    1969, oil with silver and gold leaf, on canvas
    40 x 50, signed and dated lower right
    [Plate, page 94]

87. Ethereal
    1969, oil on canvas
    45 x 30, signed and dated lower right
    [Color plate, page 80]

88. Genesis
    1969, oil with silver and gold leaf, on 4 canvases
    20 x 50 each canvas, 80 x 50 overall, signed
    and dated lower right, bottom panel
    [Color plate, page 81]

89. The L.E.M.
    1969, oil on canvas
    42 x 30, signed and dated lower right
    [Plate, page 95]

90. Watch at Night (Night Before Launch)
    1969, oil on canvas
    50 x 36, signed and dated lower right
    *Lent by National Aeronautics
    and Space Administration*
    [Color plate, page 82]

91. The White L.E.M.
    1969, oil on canvas
    40 x 30, signed and dated lower right
    [Plate, page 96]

92. Worlds
    1969, oil with lemon-gold
    and silver leaf, on canvas
    50 x 40, signed and dated lower right
    [Plate, page 97]

93. In Flight
    1963, oil on canvas
    27 x 48, signed and dated lower right
    Lent by Mr. and Mrs. Philip H. Alston, Jr.
    [Plate, page 128]

1909   Born: September 22, Fairburn, Georgia. Third of five children of Reverend Francis Jefferson and Etta Irene Cleaveland Dodd

Attended primary and elementary schools in LaGrange, Georgia. At age twelve accepted as special student in art at LaGrange College

1926   Received five-year Certificate in Art, simultaneously with diploma from LaGrange High School

1926-27   Enrolled in School of Architecture, Georgia Institute of Technology

1927-28   Instructor in Art, Five Points High School, Alabama

1928   Enrolled in Art Students League of New York. Studied with George Bridgman, Boardman Robinson; also in private classes with George Luks and Charles Martin

Exhibited watercolors in New York and Philadelphia annuals. Received favorable reviews in a joint exhibition at Anderson Galleries, New York

1930   Returned to LaGrange, Georgia to devote a year to painting
Married Mary Ridley Lehmann

1931   One-man exhibition at The High Museum of Art, Atlanta
Purchase Prize in Watercolor, Southern States Art League's 11th Annual Exhibition
Returned to Art Students League. Studied with Jean Charlot, John Steuart Curry, and former League instructors
Held first New York one-man exhibition at Ferargil Galleries

1934   Returned to the South. Managed art supply store in Birmingham for next three years, painting at night

1936	Norman Wait Harris Award, Art Institute of Chicago's 47th Annual Exhibition of American Painting and Sculpture
1937	Guest Artist, Colorado Springs Fine Arts Center (summer) Ten-year retrospective exhibition presented in Birmingham Appointed to faculty of The University of Georgia in Athens
1938	Named head of the Art Department at the University. Active in educational, civic, and professional groups; served on regional and national juries Spent summer at South Carolina and Georgia beaches, drawing and painting Special Award in Portraiture, 7th Annual Southern Art Exhibition, New York
1939	Selected as one of 13 outstanding American artists; career featured in radio series by NBC
1940	First Award, Blanche D. Benjamin Prize, Southern States Art League's 20th Annual Exhibition Second Prize for Oil Painting, International Business Machine Corporation's 'Contemporary Arts of the United States' Exhibition, New York World's Fair First acquisition by Metropolitan Museum of Art (*Sand, Sea and Sky*)
1941	Second New York one-man exhibition, Ferargil Galleries One-man exhibition, Corcoran Gallery Second Purchase Award, Association of Georgia Artists' 12th Annual Exhibition Painting of Month Award, Telfair Academy of Arts and Sciences, Savannah Daughter, Mary Irene, born
1942	Visiting Professor of Art, University of Southern California, Los Angeles, summer. Travelled in Southwest. Exhibited on West coast Elected to Graduate Faculty, University of Georgia McGregor Prize, Southern States Art League's 22nd Annual Exhibition
1944	President, Association of Georgia Artists
1945-46	Fine Arts Lecturer, Association of American Colleges; mid-West tour
1946	President, Southeastern Arts Association

1947	Honorary L.H.D. degree, LaGrange College
	Citation, Atlanta Branch, National League of American PenWomen
	Second Prize in Painting, Pepsi-Cola Company's Fourth Annual 'Paintings of the Year' Exhibition, New York
1948	Named Regents Professor of Art, University of Georgia
	Director, Artists Equity
	President, Southern States Art League
	Special Mention in Oil Painting, 3rd Southeastern Annual Exhibition of the High Museum of Art
	Edward S. Shorter Prize for Oil Painting, 19th Annual Exhibition, Association of Georgia Artists
	Purchase Prize, The Sixth Biennial Exhibition, 'Contemporary American Paintings 1948,' Virginia Museum of Fine Arts, Richmond
	Achievement Award and Medal, Honorable Mention in Painting, Pepsi-Cola Company's Fifth Annual 'Paintings of the Year' Exhibition, New York
1949	Awarded Carnegie Grant-in-Aid for research in painting
	First Purchase Prize for Watercolor, 4th Southeastern Annual Exhibition of the High Museum of Art
	Subject of feature article in *Life* magazine
	Third and fourth one-man exhibitions in New York, at Luyber Galleries
1950	Awarded Carnegie Grant-in-Aid
	Carnegie Lecturer in the Fine Arts, University of Illinois, March
	Received Grant for Painting, National Institute of Arts and Letters and the American Academy of Arts and Letters, New York
	Elected director, College Art Association of America

1951   Fine Arts Lecturer for Association of American Colleges (in Southwest)
Elected to Phi Kappa Phi, University of Georgia
Second acquisition by Metropolitan Museum of Art (*Monhegan Theme*)
Third acquisition by International Business Machines Corporation (*Drying Out*)
Awarded Carnegie Grant-in-Aid

1952   Associate Academician, National Academy of Design (A.N.A.)
One-man exhibition, Grand Central Moderns, New York
Grumbacher Art Teacher's Award in Painting, Florida International Art Exhibition
Honorable Mention in Painting, Terry National Art Exhibit, Miami

1953   One-man exhibition, Grand Central Moderns, New York
Edwin Palmer Memorial Prize, 128th Annual Exhibition, National Academy of Design, New York
Second Award, 24th Annual Exhibition, Association of Georgia Artists
First Award for Transparent Watercolor, 8th Southeastern Annual Exhibition of the High Museum of Art
Visiting Scholar for Richmond Area University Center
Received grant of $10,000 from the General Education Board of the Rockefeller Foundation, for travel and study abroad. Sailed for Europe in November, spent remainder of year in Italy

1954   Continued European travel in Italy, Spain, France, Germany, Switzerland, Belgium, Denmark, Netherlands, England, and Scotland. Returned to United States in June
One-man exhibition, Grand Central Moderns, New York
Elected president, College Art Association of America (first painter to hold the office)
Bronze Medal for Painting, Annual Exhibition of American Oil Painting, National Arts Club, New York
Honorable Mention for Watercolor, Members' Annual Exhibition, National Arts Club
National Academician, National Academy of Design (N.A.)
Charter member, Fine Arts Commission of Georgia
Member of Council, Committee on Art Education, Museum of Modern Art

1955	One-man exhibition, Grand Central Moderns, New York
	Reelected president, College Art Association of America
	Appointed Specialist to USIS Centers, Department of State
	Named director, Study of the Arts of the United States, under auspices of Carnegie Corporation of New York

1956	On leave-of-absence from University of Georgia, lectured in universities and USIS centers in Germany, Denmark, Netherlands, Turkey, Austria, Greece and Italy
	One-man exhibition of watercolors and drawings in Kassel, Germany; Istanbul and Ankara, Turkey; Vienna, Austria
	Gave lecture at National Gallery of Art
	Purchase Award, 66th Annual Exhibition, Nebraska Art Association
	Elected vice-president, College Art Association, following two terms as president

1957	Appointed charter member, U.S. Advisory Committee on the Arts
	Distinguished Service Award, Georgia State College for Women
	One-man exhibition, Grand Central Moderns, New York

1958	Purchase Award, 153rd Annual Exhibition of Paintings and Sculpture, The Pennsylvania Academy of Fine Arts
	Purchase Award, Fourth International Hallmark Art Award Competition
	Special Mention in Oil Painting, 13th Southeastern Annual Exhibition of the High Museum of Art, Atlanta
	Two-month tour of Russia and Far East, as envoy for U.S. Department of State; on the first Cultural Exchange between the United States and USSR; as guest of Soviet government toured USSR. Continued as U.S. Specialist to USIS Centers: India, Thailand, Philippine Islands, Japan, Korea, and Hawaii

1959	Honorary D.F.A. degree, University of Chattanooga
	Member, Citizens' Advisory Committee for the American National Exhibition in Moscow
	Committee on the Visual Arts in Higher Education, for Ford Foundation and College Art Association of America
	Third Award, 5th 'Painting of the Year' Exhibition, Mead Corporation, Atlanta

1960	One-man exhibition, Grand Central Moderns, New York
	Coordinated the Visual Arts programs for the USIS 'Forum' series for broadcast over Voice
	of America network to Latin America, Europe, Africa, Near East, Far East, and South Asia
	Member, National Council of the Arts and Government
	Chairman of Jury of Selections for Fulbright Awards in Painting for 1960-61

1961   Appointed chairman of Division of Fine Arts, The University of Georgia
Reappointed chairman of Jury Selections for Fulbright Awards in Painting for 1961-62
Served as member Committee for International Cultural Exchange; Committee on
Government in Art
Reappointed for third term to United States Advisory Committee on the Arts
Featured subject of 'Meet the Professor' in first of a series of television interviews:
ABC-TV, New York

1962   One-man exhibition, Grand Central Moderns, New York
Received Painting of Distinction Award, 'Painting of the Year' Exhibition,
Mead Corporation, Atlanta
Named director, National Council of the Arts in Education

1963   Visiting Scholar for the United Chapters of Phi Beta Kappa for 1963-64
Designated official NASA artist for Mercury Astronaut-9 project; selected to cover Gordon
Cooper's orbital spacecraft launching at Cape Canaveral

1964   One-man exhibition, Grand Central Moderns, New York
Arthur Harris Award of Merit, 34th Annual Exhibition of the Association of Georgia Artists
The Hodgson-Dodd fund established by friends in honor of Hugh Hodgson and Lamar
Dodd, with $50,000 corpus 'to give practical recognition to the departments of music and
art' at The University of Georgia

1965   Exhibited at National Gallery of Art, Washington, in 'Eyewitness to Space' exhibition by
NASA artists
One-man exhibition, Grand Central Moderns, New York

1966   Awarded Gold Medal for Meritorious Services by Georgia Society, Sons of the
American Revolution
Visiting Scholar for United Chapters of Phi Beta Kappa for 1966-67
Consultant for International Humanities Program, McGill University, Montreal
and University of Toronto

1967   One-man exhibition, Grand Central Moderns, New York

1968   Honorary D.F.A. degree, Florida State University
NASA artist for launching of Apollo 7, Cape Kennedy

1969   NASA artist for launching of Apollo 10, Cape Kennedy and Apollo 11,
Houston Manned Spacecraft Center
Exhibited paintings on space themes at National Gallery of Art, Washington

1970   Elected Fellow of the Royal Society of Arts, London (F.R.S.A.)

A Selection of Critical Commentary

About the Artist's Work Spanning the Period 1939-1969.

Ethel Hutson
Sunday Item-Tribune,
New Orleans
March 5, 1939

Whether he paints twisted trees or sand dunes, a window open into the night or a portrait, or sketches the streets of New York or the beaches of the Georgia coast, Lamar Dodd is alive, dynamic, and yet holds his powers in a restraint which is curiously sober for so young a painter.

Art Digest
March, 1940

Dodd, whose palette has become more subtle since his first New York showing in 1933, turns a sympathetic eye on the landscape out of which springs Athens, home city of the University of Georgia. His *View of Athens*, a soundly integrated composition in which railroad tracks and roads weave under and over each other, rings out with a quiet which the clatter of a distant train fails to disrupt. In the rear, on the summit of a slope, the buildings of Athens jut up out of a band of foliage, and overhead a dramatic sky sends down an opulent warmth that permeates the entire scene.

Emily Genauer
*New York
World-Telegram*
June 15, 1940

Lamar Dodd's *Sand, Sea and Sky* is an interesting piece. It's a small canvas, a study of low dunes, heavy skies, tall wind-bent grasses. But in the undulating, wavelike forms of the sand, the curve of the vegetation, the paths of the parallel serpentine brushwork, and the low, almost monochromatic palette, are turbulence and force.

Marion Wright
Charlotte Observer
April 6, 1941

His painting is noted primarily for technical excellence. He has a way of coaxing beauty from neutral colors and tones, arranged ever so casually but with grace and charm, as in *Still Life-Magnolias*. The flowers are the contrasting notes that nestle like pearls amidst the browns of the cloth, the pine burrs and needles, against a grayish brown background. Fine draftsmanship is another prime quality in his work, clearly evident in the picture under discussion.

[J.W.L.] *Art News*
November 15, 1941

Where Brook would be sad and dreary, Dodd draws the subject similarly but fires it with shimmer, color and significance.

Edward Alden Jewell *New York Times* Sunday, November 16, 1941	This artist seems at his best when he restricts color almost to monotone. There is great richness here.
Florence S. Berryman *Sunday Star*, Washington January 4, 1942	Despite an education in art under such painters as Richard Lahey, Boardman Robinson, Jean Charlot, John Steuart Curry (one of the original 'American Scene Trinity'), George Bridgman and George Luks, Mr. Dodd avoided becoming a carbon copy of any of them. His style is his own. . . .
Jean Charlot in Catalog Foreword to Lamar Dodd's Exhibition at Agnes Scott College, February, 1944	One will find in his work as a whole that cotton pickers and picturesque sights are rather the exception. What he portrays of Georgia is a more elusive and deeper quality, a turn of mind, a design for living, that may seem clannish to outsiders, but is rich in rewards for those born to it; perhaps a compound of tradition and reserve, an Eighteenth Century cast of manners, a musqueteer [sic] belief in the innate nobility of amateurism that never allows one to confuse a job with life itself, however excellent, or proficient, or successful one may be at it.
Rosamund Frost *Art News* April 1-14, 1945	. . . Lamar Dodd's powerful *Madonnas of the Rain* gives back to the human figure the dignity it elsewhere lacks.
Ralph M. Pearson *Art Digest* April 15, 1947	Likewise the people of Georgia have improved on the art educational techniques of some of their fellows. For instance, in contrast to our docile tolerance of the incredibly reactionary Art Syllabus of the State of New York, they place a well-earned confidence in an artist, Mr. Lamar Dodd. Results in eager interest of children and adults are impressive.
Edward Alden Jewell *New York Times* Sunday, October 5, 1947	*The Breaker*, by Lamar Dodd, which received the second highest award of $2,000, is splendid and should have been designated tops instead of the very dubious 'Country Tenement' by Henry Kallen. . . .
Margaret Breuning *Art Digest* January 15, 1949	Dodd is a realist in that he finds his inspiration in his environing world, but his translation of his personal reactions to it reveal his subtle perception of the character of his visual experiences and of the relation of the things observed to one another. One gains the sensation from this work that it was inevitable, that is to say that the effects could not be gained in any other way. It is, perhaps, the simplicity and directness of his statements that indicate the artist's knowledge of the exact requirements of each theme.
Judith Kaye Reed *Art Digest* October 1, 1949	Because Dodd's large oils are vigorous organizations of form and color it is doubly interesting to see his works in less formal mediums and to learn that his approach here is as sure, as swift-seeming and as direct.

New York Sun October 7, 1949	Lamar Dodd, who also knows something about getting down to fundamentals, unashamedly and purposefully plays on the emotions, as a musician plays on his harp strings. There is thunder in his skies, threat in his seas, and peace in his fields. Dodd's watercolors of the sea have the strength of simplicity, in color and form, and an unceasing rhythm of movement perfectly controlled in both gentleness and force.
New York Times October 7, 1949	Always a strong colorist, Dodd relies on a narrow dark range to emphasize properly the stern statements made about nature in these works. Stormy skies, wind-swept seas, leafless trees—such are the uncompromising elements that are built into his pictures. And in no case does the artist make concessions to charm or picturesqueness as such. Dodd's is a clear and consistent vision.
Carlyle Burrows *New York* *Herald Tribune* Sunday, October 9, 1949	In this show Mr. Dodd takes in the appearance of the landscape with utmost economy of means, simplifying much and defining the rugged contours of the seacoast, great trees and abrupt vistas of ocean and sky with impressionistic ease and directness. The form that he induces in his work leaves us with strong impressions of trees, drawn very much as Cézanne would have drawn them. Dodd's work is already known; but the drawings give us a fresh and intimate view of his ability and feeling for natural scenes and objects.
Alice Lawton *Boston Post* Sunday, October 30, 1949	A bold and vigorous brush . . . Mr. Dodd includes a few well-chosen Northern landscapes, along with his predominately Southern works. They are of Monhegan, Maine, and Rockport, Massachusetts, both New England Art meccas. . . .
Edgar J. Driscoll, Jr. *Boston Sunday Globe* October 30, 1949	A handsome collection of paintings. Dodd paints in a forceful vigorous manner, skillfully creating moods. His color is sound, his draftsmanship is of top-drawer caliber, and the manner in which he lays on his pigment lends an added note of authority to his work.
Lawrence Dame *Boston Herald* Sunday, October 30, 1949	Painting mostly in oil, Dodd achieves highly dramatic effects with well-chosen elements of landscape. He is a colorist who can be immensely effective in low key, fond of contrast and silhouetted shapes, possessed of a great feeling for rhythm and texture. You sense his vigor throughout this large show. Sometimes, as in his Monhegan studies, he seems to reveal influences of Marin and Hartley, since he goes abstract in depicting torrents of white for waves jelled over symbolic rocks. His use of planes is admirable for the rugged qualities he wishes to impart to nature. Now and then his palette springs aflame, as in his flowering peach orchard in which a very loose technique is effective, and in his cotton pickers, where the figures, bent over cruelly, symbolize subtly the pangs of toil on an earth which should be rich for all. His still lifes are masterly in their ability to express much with little. . . .

Wendell F. Zoehler
Your Weekly Guide to Boston
November 5, 1949

He is a man of prodigious energy and production. He paints with a vigorous style. With almost abandon he overcomes technical difficulties of magnitude and brings a complex array of subject material into coherent design and Ryder-like moody expressiveness. He uses the palette knife as surely as the brush, dramatic and telling in swirl or stroke. His attitude towards nature is that of a post-impressionist. His ability to organize and express through form and color the aesthetic values inherent in nature and enhance as poignantly as possible their essential characteristics is impressive. His mind at times seems to seek a mystic value behind nature especially in his more dramatic, brooding canvases.

Carl Holty
Banner-Herald,
Athens, Georgia
November 18, 1949

Here we find the same poetry so characteristic of his early industrial landscapes. It is good to see the quality revived from time to time. For as a painter passes from one period of his interest to another and as he develops new methods, it is of vital importance that all his discoveries and all the facets of his talent be absorbed into his personality. In *Drying Out*, a small canvas, Dodd achieves another kind of poetry in the plastic language of the paint itself. The resilient strength of the light colors and the delicacy of the painting are not dependent here, as in the larger green *Springtime*, upon the motive itself but emanate directly from the artist's vision.

Pictures on Exhibit
February, 1952

Lamar Dodd is probably at his strongest in those paintings which are organized around facades from which volumes have been subtracted, at least in the artist's mind. Thus, recesses in a quarry tell of stone removed, or a flight of stairs recedes from a vertical plane. Cézanne, of course, distilled such effects from materials in his native Provence, and it is this tailoring of chimerical volumes which places Dodd in the classicist-intellectual tradition. Aside from his flexible Cubist framework and technical competence, there are also romantic manifestations in cool chalky colors sometimes built up into a moderate impasto.

[H.L.F.] *Art News*
February, 1952

It is more the general effect and the handling rather than the actual form that are expressionist. Actually many of Dodd's motifs tend toward disciplined cadences of abstract rhythmic movement. Towering chasms of skyscrapers and abandoned quarries are almost interchangeable in their gridwork of vertical and horizontal patches; seascapes seem like the codified rendering of twisting wave-forms and angular rocks; and the repeated diagonals of bending figures in *Cotton Pickers*, like the conscious evocation of an Egyptian bas-relief. That they are more than mere exercises in design is evident from the personal colors which activate an interplay of planes and masses, achieving notable unity in *Nature's Monuments*.

<table>
<tr>
<td>

Margaret Breuning
Art Digest
February 1, 1952

</td>
<td>

In *Triton's Cove*, Dodd conveys a momentary aspect of the crushing weight of moving water in its resistance to the rocky shore. A fine perception of volume and space permits him to include the informal vastness of the sea, the recession of the shore line, the depths of blue sky in a plastic design of dynamic power that far exceeds any literal description of the scene.

</td>
</tr>
<tr>
<td>

New York Times
Sunday,
February 3, 1952

</td>
<td>

His sea-pieces carry a Marinesque brusqueness over into something very substantial. Knife-blades of paint are applied to the canvas in an air of high excitement, which is in keeping with the bounding waves and the storm-beaten rocks. This pace is slowed down for a scene in the swamps, in which mists of green hang over the vegetation and the stifling vista.

As a designer he appears at his strongest, perhaps, in the pattern of triangles that he encloses his *Cotton Pickers* and in the handsomely balanced group of tug-boats in a port. He has made something very striking of the criss-crossing of spars, and sterns and bows.

</td>
</tr>
<tr>
<td>

Carlyle Burrows
*New York
Herald Tribune*
Sunday,
February 3, 1952

</td>
<td>

Mr. Dodd brings to the Grand Central Moderns a group of paintings that add to his stature as a romantic impressionist. Especially in respect to the feeling with which he paints the seacoast, the woods and other subjects whose stark forms loom with a mysterious grandeur in his work, ranging from Maine to the cotton fields of Georgia, does this artist affirm what is most essential, both as to form and spirit. In painting of this kind, the simplicity is a deceptive note and can be ascribed to easy gestures. But not so, I think, with Mr. Dodd, who like Marin conveys in his brooding landscape much of the finer spirit of his subject with simple means.

</td>
</tr>
<tr>
<td>

Leslie Judd Portner
Washington Post
Sunday, April 6, 1952

</td>
<td>

The painting is architectural in its handling of built-up masses of rock, churning seas and clouded skies. The brushwork is often reminiscent of Cézanne, as is the analysis of the structural forms of nature, especially as seen in the landscape, *Nature's Monuments*. There is no misunderstanding the very firm foundation on which the work is based, nor the artist's ability to handle paint. This is painting in the classic tradition, yet with a clear understanding of the abstract elements in nature.

</td>
</tr>
<tr>
<td>

Allan Bryant
*Atlanta Journal and
Constitution Magazine*
November 23, 1954

</td>
<td>

In all of these new works Mr. Dodd has carried forward 'the maturity in development of the simplification of ideas,' noted by so many writers and critics at his latest one-man show.

</td>
</tr>
<tr>
<td>

Howard Devree
New York Times
Sunday,
November 6, 1955

</td>
<td>

Dodd has returned from Italy with heightened color in his paintings, with Mediterranean light suffusing the facades of age old cathedrals and with new vitality and light in these impressions without abandoning the sound structure underlying his frankly more picturesque themes.

</td>
</tr>
</table>

Tagespost, Linz, Austria
April, 1956
Professor Dodd's work as a painter, honored with many prizes and continuously exhibited in American galleries of art, rests upon maturity of thought and power of feeling. One might be tempted to say that his profile as an artist is based on a strongly architectural way of seeing which expresses the immediacy of his subjects, be it a narrow street in the big city or the 'Elevated' in New York with towering skyscrapers in the background.

Stuart Preston
New York Times
Sunday,
October 27, 1957
Lamar Dodd's latest semi-abstractions, at Grand Central Moderns, embody a pictorial report of a Mediterranean sojourn. Dodd is cagey with his subject matter, never going after it head on, but catching its flavor and look in one or more oblique ways. In some of these delicate impressions of Venice and the Italian hill towns he seems to prefer a fashionable artistic convention to a spontaneous reaction to a scene. But in others he translates what he sees into a fresh, slightly fantastic variation of itself. Needless to say, the Gothic extravagance of Venetian palaces appeals to his esthetic eye. On the other hand, the skyline of Constantinople is set down with maximum terseness not at all exempt from a true sense of the picturesque.

Frank Getlein
Sunday Star,
Washington
March 14, 1965
Lamar Dodd is seen in an eerie interior of a capsule with astronaut, the supine figure all but lost in the dials and levers around him; and a Piranesi-like view of a gantry interior, looking down from level to level surrounding the great cylinder.

Edmund Burke Feldman
*Atlanta Journal
and Constitution*
Sunday,
November 19, 1967
The artist's contact with urban vistas tends to be lyrical rather than tragic. Even the lustrous, dark, *Over and Beyond*, with its dusky eventide effects, strains for a quiet serenity where we have lately been accustomed to think of suffering and violence.

Edmund Burke Feldman
*Atlanta Journal
and Constitution*
Sunday,
November 16, 1969
Dodd has been fascinated, for some years, by the view of the land as seen from the sky, from approaching aircraft, from the visual standpoint of the air passenger who is about to make the transition from the bouyant uncluttered upper atmosphere into the maelstrom of social and mechanical energy orbits that constitute the ambience of a typical American metropolis like Atlanta.

It appears that Lamar Dodd has made a determined effort to represent the visual and, one might say, the poetic experience of men standing many thousands of miles outside the earth and looking back upon it as persons who are at once infinitely detached and yet very much of the earth. In other words, he has attempted to define visually the experience of moving out of a world and back into it. He portrays a variety of moods and attitudes from the standpoint of the spacemen, and from the standpoint of the earthlings who stay behind and watch and wonder.

Representation in Major Collections

Addison Gallery of American Art, Phillips Academy, *Andover, Massachusetts*

Birmingham Museum of Art, *Alabama*

C.I.T. Financial Corporation, *New York*

College of Wooster Art Center, *Wooster, Ohio*

The Columbus Gallery of Fine Arts, *Ohio*

The Columbus Museum of Arts and Crafts, *Georgia*

The Container Corporation of America, *Chicago*

Contemporary Art Collection, Atlanta University

Cranbrook Academy of Art, Bloomfield Hills, *Michigan*

Davenport Municipal Art Gallery, *Iowa*

Georgia Museum of Art, The University of Georgia, *Athens*

Grand Rapids Art Museum, *Michigan*

Hallmark Collection, Kansas City, *Missouri*

The High Museum of Art, *Atlanta*

The International Business Machines Corporation, *New York*

Lehigh University, Bethlehem, *Pennsylvania*

The Mead Corporation, *Atlanta*

Memorial Art Gallery of The University of Rochester, *New York*

The Metropolitan Museum of Art, *New York*

The Montclair Art Museum, Montclair, *New Jersey*

The National Academy of Design, *New York*

The National Aeronautics and Space Administration, *Washington*

National Collection of Fine Arts, The Smithsonian Institution, *Washington*

The Nebraska Art Association, Sheldon Memorial Art Gallery,
    University of Nebraska, *Lincoln*

The Pennsylvania Academy of the Fine Arts, *Philadelphia*

San Jose State College, San Jose, *California*

Spelman College, *Atlanta*

Telfair Academy of Arts and Sciences, *Savannah*

University of Notre Dame Art Gallery, *South Bend, Indiana*

The Virginia Museum of Fine Arts, *Richmond*

Andrew Dickson White Museum of Art, Cornell University, Ithaca, *New York*

The Whitney Museum of American Art, *New York*

Wilmington Society of the Fine Arts, Delaware Art Center, *Wilmington*

A Selected Bibliography

Books, Articles, and Reviews

Breuning, Margaret: In 'Art in New York.' *Parnassus*, v.9, December, 1937, pp.23, 26. 1 il.

Boswell, Peyton: 'As the Bough Is Bent' [Editorial]. *Art Digest,* v.13, November 15, 1938, p.3.

Unsigned: 'Lamar Dodd.' *Sketch Book of Kappa Pi,* v.4, Spring, 1938, p.28.

Unsigned: In 'For the New York World's Fair.' *Parnassus,* v.11, March, 1939, pp.15, 16. 1 il.

Boswell, Peyton: In 'Four Stars!' [Editorial]. *Art Digest*, v.13, September 1, 1939, p.26.

Unsigned: In 'Resident Apostle.' *Time*, v.34, September 18, 1939, p.56.

Watson, Forbes, *American Painting Today*. Washington: American Federation of Arts, 1939, pp.68, 105, 335. 1 il.

Cheney, Martha Candler, *Modern Art in America*. New York: McGraw-Hill, 1939, pp.71,148. 1 il.

Boswell, Peyton: In 'New York Fair Holds First Regional Preview.' *Art Digest*, v.13, January 1, 1939, p.20. 1 il.

Childers, James Saxon: 'Georgia Artist.' *Magazine of Sigma Chi*, v.59, February, 1940, pp.46-56. 8 ils.

Unsigned: 'Lamar Dodd Comes Up from the Deep South.' *Art Digest*, v.14, March 1, 1940, p.16. 1 il.

Unsigned: In 'American Challenge.' *Time*, v.35, March 11, 1940, p.57.

Unsigned: 'Lamar Dodd.' *Magazine of Art*, v.33, April, 1940, pp.227, 231. 1 il.

Boswell, Peyton: 'Dodd of Georgia' [Editorial]. *Art Digest*, v.14, April 15, 1940, p.27.

Watson, Jane: In 'News and Comment.' *Magazine of Art*, v.33, November, 1940, pp.640-5, 649-50, 654-5. 1 il.

Unsigned: 'The Deep South As Seen by Lamar Dodd.' *Art Digest*, v.16, November 15, 1941, p.10. 1 il.

Wheeler, Monroe, *Painters and Sculptors of Modern America*. New York: Crowell, 1942, pp.26-30. 5 ils.

Watson, Jane: 'Exhibition: Lamar Dodd, Corcoran Gallery.' *Magazine of Art*, v.35, January, 1942, p.47.

Crane, W.M., Jr.: 'Lamar Dodd, Foremost Southern Painter.' *The Southern Literary Messenger*, v.4, December, 1942, pp.467-9. 2 ils.

Boswell, Peyton, Jr.: 'Southern Artist Scores at Carnegie Exhibition.' *Art Digest*, v.19, October 15, 1944, pp.6,7. 1 il.

Unsigned: 'Lamar Dodd.' *The Southerner*. New Orleans: Southern Editors Association, 1944, p.148; 1945, pp.156-7.

Thomas, Howard: 'Lamar Dodd, Southern Painter.' *American Artist*, v.10, February, 1946, pp.8-13. 4 ils.

Lansford, Alonzo: In 'Virginia Biennial.' *Art Digest*, v. 22, May 1, 1948, pp.9, 32. 1 il.

Mack, Walter S., Jr.: In 'Southern Artists and Pepsi-Cola's Art Programs.' *Southern Advertising and Publishing*, June 15, 1948, pp.32-5. 1 il.

Bethers, Ray, *Composition in Pictures*. New York: Pitman, 1949, pp.12, 13. 2 ils.

Larkin, Oliver W., *Art and Life in America*. New York: Holt, Rinehart and Winston, 1949, rev.ed. 1960, p.415.

Breuning, Margaret: 'The Dynamic Power of Lamar Dodd.' *Art Digest*, v.23, January 15, 1949, cover, p.12. 2 ils.

Varga, Margit: 'In An Un-Bohemian Way He Sparks an Art Movement in the South.' *Life*, v.27, September 26, 1949, pp.62-7. 7 ils.

Boswell, Peyton, Jr.: In 'University of Georgia Enriched.' *Art Digest*, v.23, March 1, 1949, p.12.

Graves, Maitland, *The Art of Color and Design*. New York: McGraw-Hill, 1951, p.5.

Bethers, Ray, *How Paintings Happen*. New York: Norton, 1951, p.77. 1 il.

Cheney, Sheldon, *The Story of Modern Art*. New York: Viking Press, 1951, pp.55, 626. 1 il. rev.ed. 1958, pp.604, 628, 661. 1 il.

Pousette-Dart, Nathaniel, *American Art and Artists*. New York: Pellegrini & Cudahy, 1953. 1 il.

Thieme, Ulrich and Becker, Felix, *Allegemeines Lexikon der Bildenden Künstler*. Leipzig: Seeman, 1953; 1908-1947, v.1, p.574.

Smith, Lillian, *The Journey*. New York: World, 1954, pp.136-8.

Davidson, Martha: 'Lamar Dodd: Artist-Educator-Administrator.' *American Artist*, v.20. February, 1956, pp.22-7, 63-4. 9 ils.

Bethers, Ray, *Style in Painting*. New York: Hastings, 1957, p.87. 1 il.

Watson, Ernest, *Composition in Landscape and Still Life*. New York: Watson-Guptill, 1956, pp.67-8, 81, 83-4, 106, 199. 2 ils.

Pierson, William H., Jr. and Davidson, Martha, eds., *Arts of the United States: A Pictorial Survey*. New York: McGraw-Hill, 1960. In John I.H. Baur: 'Painting of the Twentieth Century.' pp.80, 338. Reprinted Athens, University of Georgia Press, 1966. 1 il.

The American Library Compendium and Index of World Art. New York: Noble, 1961, p.225.

Hurd, Peter: In 'Countdown at Canaveral.' *Art in America*, v.51, October, 1963, p.72. 1 il. Reprinted in *Mercury Atlas-9*, Washington: National Aeronautics and Space Administration, 1963.

Unsigned: 'Lamar Dodd's New Works.' *Art News*, v.64, November, 1965, p.13.

C.T.: 'Lamar Dodd,' In 'In the Galleries.' *Arts*, v.42, November, 1967, p.55.

Unsigned: In 'Artists Capture Marvel of Space Flights.' *Panorama*, Maracaibo, Domingo, December 14, 1969, p.9. 1 il.

Feldman, Edmund Burke, *Becoming Human Through Art*. New York: Prentice-Hall, 1970. 3 ils. [unpaged.]

93. In Flight

Lent by Mr. and Mrs. Philip H. Alston, Jr.

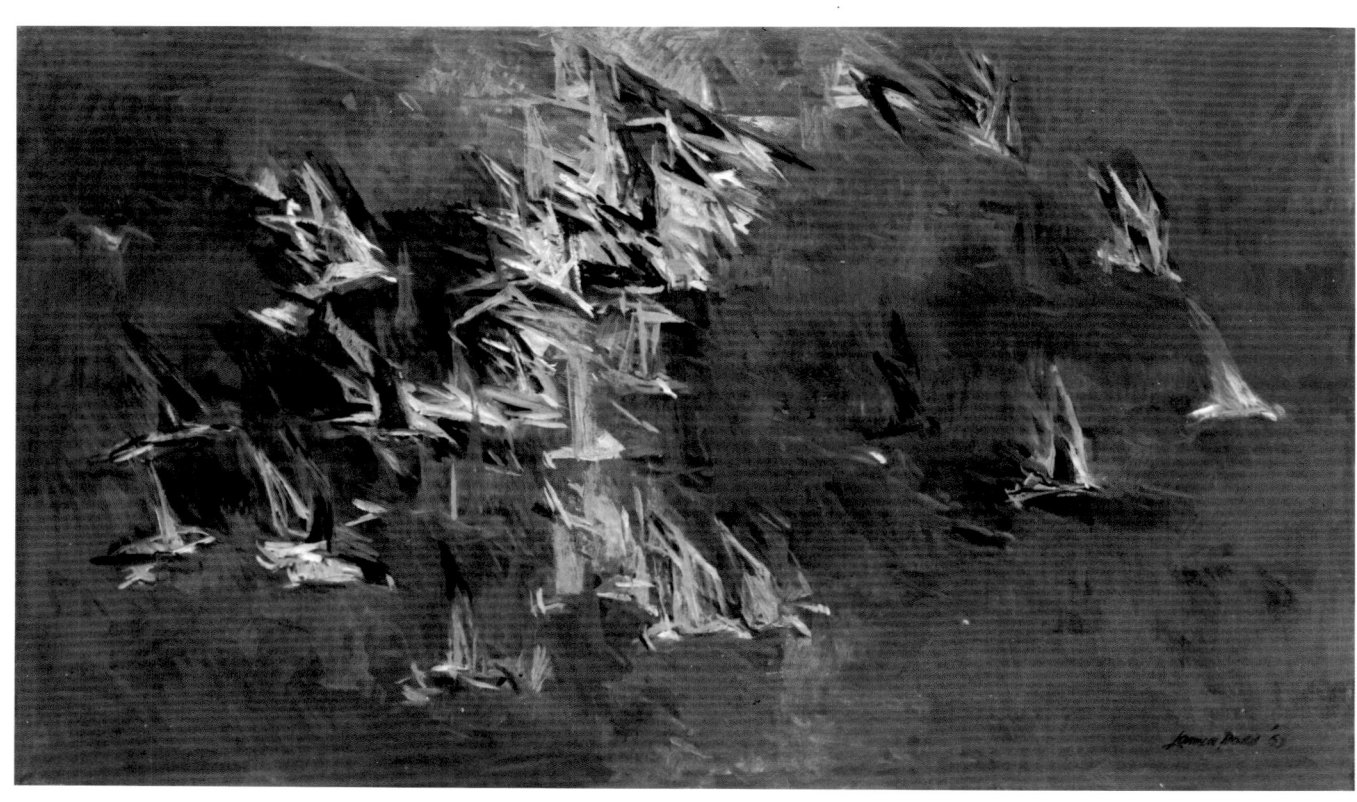

Fred C. Davison
President
The University
of Georgia

This catalogue simply marks a milestone in the life of one of this country's distinguished artists and citizens. We all await with even greater expectations that which we know will follow.

Lamar Dodd   Past, present, and future...To many I owe so very much.

Index of the Catalogue

Photographic Credits

All color and black and white photographs are by the team of
W. Robert Nix and *Wiley D. Sanderson, Jr.*, Athens, Georgia,
except the following:

Oliver Baker, New York, pp.58, 75
Jerome Drown, Atlanta 77
Kenneth Kay, Athens, Georgia 30-2, 34, 43, 45, 47-50, 52-3, 57
Andrew Moore, Allentown, Pennsylvania 61
Phillips Studio, Philadelphia 73
Gene Pyle, Athens, Georgia 9
Robinson Studios, Grand Rapids 69
Frank J. Thomas, Los Angeles 46
Courtesy Addison Gallery of American Art 91
Courtesy Fogg Art Museum, Harvard University 63
Courtesy Memorial Art Gallery, University of Rochester 44
Courtesy The Metropolitan Museum of Art 55
Courtesy National Aeronautics and Space Administration 82, 84
Courtesy The Nebraska Art Association,
    Sheldon Memorial Art Gallery, University of Nebraska 66
Courtesy Virginia Museum of Fine Arts 51